WHAT'S BREWING IN NEW ENGLAND

A Guide to Brewpubs and Craft Breweries

KATE CONE

Camden, Maine

Down East Books

Published by Down East Books
An imprint of Globe Pequot
Trade Division of The Rowman & Littlefield Publishing Group, Inc.
4501 Forbes Boulevard, Suite 200, Lanham, Maryland 20706
www.rowman.com

Unit A, Whitacre Mews, 26-34 Stannary Street, London SE11 4AB, United Kingdom

British Library Cataloguing in Publication Information Available

Library of Congress Cataloging-in-Publication Data Available

ISBN 978-1-60893-395-2 (paperback)
ISBN 978-1-60893-396-9 (e-book)

∞™ The paper used in this publication meets the minimum requirements of American National Standard for Information Sciences—Permanence of Paper for Printed Library Materials, ANSI/NISO Z39.48-1992.

To my dad, Clinton Francis "Kip" Cone Sr.,
who knew things like why there are holes in saltines, why you should drink
your Bourbon neat, and why you should not go gentle into that good night

Contents

Foreword

Drinking locally—before there was anything local to drink
By Al Diamon

Being a beer drinker in Maine used to be hard work.

Well, not the actual drinking part. That's always been pretty easy. But finding good beer to drink could be a real chore.

Before Three Dollar Dewey's alehouse opened its doors on Fore Street in Portland in 1980, the selection in most bars and stores in the state could best be described as grim. You might find a place with a few dusty bottles of Guinness stout in stock. Every now and then, a couple six-packs of Heineken Dark (shudder) would get shipped here accidentally. I knew a place that would special order the original Ballantine India Pale Ale (aged in real oak kegs)—if you were willing to buy an entire case. In late winter, both Narragansett and Pabst put out semi-credible bock beers. And friends traveling from such exotic locations as San Francisco and Wisconsin could sometimes be persuaded to bring back samples of Anchor Steam or Point Special.

But most days, when beer o'clock rolled around, I drank whatever met my exacting criterion of being the cheapest stuff available. If I had to settle for bland, indifferent swill, at least I wasn't going to pay much for it. Even after Dewey's began transforming the scene with its vast selection of exotic imports and quirky survivors of America's repeated attempts to stamp out all distinctive brews, I still tended to gravitate toward the inexpensive.

While I was delighted and enlightened to sample a range of British bitters, German pilsners, and Belgian ales that tasted like nothing I'd ever imagined could be called beer, I was still on a limited budget, one that wouldn't allow for many of what seemed like outrageously priced two-dollar pints or four-dollar bottles. Not when an entire quart of Ballantine Triple X could be had for a mere buck.

But gradually, my bias toward quantity over quality began to erode. While I still kept my refrigerator stocked with a six-pack of Green Death pounders (for the uninitiated, that was our affectionate nickname for Ballantine's olive-hued 16-ounce cans), it sometimes had to share shelf space with a few bottles of the venerable Bass Pale Ale or the upstart Samuel Adams Boston Lager.

But I wasn't drinking anything local, because there wasn't anything local to drink. Maine hadn't had a commercial brewery since well before Prohibition. It wasn't clear whether such an enterprise was even legally possible, let alone commercially feasible. Dewey's had created a small but dedicated consumer base for more robust, full-bodied beers, but neither state regulators nor deep-pocketed investors displayed much interest in aiding any forward-thinking entrepreneurs in exploiting that market.

If it hadn't been for the perseverance and imagination of David Geary and a few of his colleagues, I'd probably still be drinking Heineken Dark (which Geary once described as "Heineken Light with Gravy Master in it") and figuring that was going to be about as good as it got. Thanks to Geary and the other pioneers of the Maine brewing scene, I was spared that terrible fate.

Now I'm so conditioned to drinking fine, local brews that I don't experience the slightest tremor when I get charged seven bucks a pint. Well, maybe a little one.

Al Diamon writes the weekly column "Politics & Other Mistakes" for several Maine newspapers. He's also the media critic for The Bollard *magazine and the resident contrarian for* My Generation *magazine.*

Introduction

You all know about Rip Van Winkle, the character in the short story written by Washington Irving. Dude wanders off from his village, decides he needs a nap, and when he awakens, he discovers he's been asleep for 20 years, totally missing the American Revolution. I kind of feel like that guy. It's been over 20 years since I began my craft beer journey.

When I was researching and writing my first *What's Brewing in New England*, I had just finished my stint at Shipyard Brewing Company. I worked as assistant to the president, Fred Forsley. It was 1994 and the company had just begun putting together their brewery in Portland. The bulk of my job was jack of all trades and master of none. The place was so frenetic, with Alan Pugsley getting the brewing side going and Fred trying to keep the lights on, so to speak. Everyone who worked there worked several jobs—and we all loved it. I did a little legal work, some publicity for new beers, like Longfellow Ale (SBC is located on the site where the poet Henry Wadsworth Longfellow was born), and wrangling the salesmen, setting up the office with a fax machine, taking calls from customers, returning Fred's phone calls, and when we finally got it, getting our name out to the public via the Internet.

At the time, I was writing a novel, and an agent I met with one day advised, "Write a book about beer! You're in the business and it's going crazy." So I did. I wrote up a book proposal and sent my query. Down East Books called and asked to meet with me. After working out the details, it was official. I was setting down my novel and writing a book about microbrewed beer, published in 1997.

In a space of two and a half years, I proposed the book to the publisher, signed the contract, and began my journey, like ol' Rip, venturing away from my village of Harpswell, Maine, and setting off across New England to visit as many of the quickly proliferating brewpubs and microbreweries as I could. I was an explorer who talked to brewers, owners, chefs, and bartenders who had decided to "follow their bliss," as Joseph Campbell urges us humans to do, dump careers, and make beer for a living. Some of them succeeded, if you measure success by being able to keep the business going. Many of them didn't make it. The late '90s experienced a microbrew shakeout, resulting in the closing of many of the places I featured in that first book.

By the time you hold this in your hands, it will be 20 years—yes, the same two decades Rip Van Winkle slept while the rest of the village brought the king to his knees and fought for independence—since I got back into the beer scene. There has been another revolution in the beer biz, except now, we don't really say "microbrew." "Craft beer" is the term we use to describe beers made at a small scale.

There are other changes: Most of the New England states—Vermont, New Hampshire, Maine, Massachusetts, Rhode Island, and Connecticut—have altered their beverage laws and tweaked their blue laws to allow brewers to charge for samples of their beers in their tasting or tap rooms. Previously, in some states, you had to open either a brewpub, where a full-scale food-service operation existed, or a brewery. In the former, beer was sold as well as food. In the latter, tours were given and samples of beer were given away free. This may sound like a small change, but for many people opening today, it is a crucial model that will allow them to sell directly to the consumer and avoid the more complicated level of finding a distributor to take them on and represent them, i.e., sell their products enthusiastically and add the expense of having to package the beer.

Brewers today, if they choose, can have a small brewery out back and a tasting room out front. Beer lovers bring their growlers, refill them, and taste samples of the beer while they wait. Food trucks appear outside, and the brewer avoids the licensing of having to open a food operation. As this book goes to print, brewpub, bar, and restaurant owners are giving a bit of push-back, saying that the licensing fees and regulations they have to pay and comply with are far more cumbersome than those the breweries have. We'll see how it shakes out.

The venerable brewpubs still exist. Gritty McDuff's in Portland, Maine, was the first to open east of the Mississippi in the 1980s and has celebrated 25 years. But today there are more options, and therefore more opportunity, for brewers to exist successfully with a tiny brewing system and an even tinier tasting room.

What have I been doing these past 20 years? Glad you asked, because unlike Rip Van Winkle, I was doing anything but sleeping. After *What's Brewing* came out, I enjoyed doing book signings and meeting people who sometimes drove a couple of hours to meet me (wow, was I surprised, and delighted) and relaxed after writing for a long time, chasing down owners and brewers, trying to coax a few lines from them to put in the book. The book sold well, but I knew that it would be quickly outdated. That's how fast the beer scene was moving.

I wrote for *Ale Street News*; had a column for *Yankee Brew News* and our local paper, the *Brunswick Times Record*; and appeared on *The David Brudnoy* show on WBZ radio in Boston and with my former boss Fred Forsley on Portland's WCSH television. I even brewed for a day at Kennebunkport Brewing Company. I was consulted for a report on New Hampshire public radio and contributed to beer publications I'm not sure still exist (publishing is as volatile as brewing). My greatest honor came when I won a blue ribbon at the Maine Organic Farmers and Gardeners Organization (MOFGA) fair for a sweet Irish stout I had made with my own two hands (think Guinness in the thick square bottle).

And, I raised three kids on my own. So no, I wasn't napping, I was busy parenting, which I am happy for. My kids turned out great, despite the gray hairs I grew going through some of their shenanigans. Now I'm an empty nester, and trust me, that transition was not easy. I cried for two years every time the school bus roared down our road. I'm much better now.

How did I get *What's Brewing* resurrected? Good question. One day, while procrastinating writing the mystery novel I'm back to writing— one that is set in a brewpub, no less—I wondered if I might still have the rights to the beer book. I decided to approach Down East about my out-of-print book. The result is the book you now hold in your hands, a second edition, although my editor called it a "rewrite," requiring a quick tally of how many folks in my first book were no longer in business and another look at the number of new brewers listed on the Brewers Association website.

I had to sit down in my big red leather reading chair and do some deep breathing. This is a new creation. There are 200 breweries or brewpubs in the six New England states, and more opening every day. Just in the year I've been doing research, at least five places opened in Maine alone. The Brewers Association announced in July 2014 that the number of craft breweries in the United States topped 3,000 and 1.2 breweries open each day. As we go to print, that number has topped 4,200 and is climbing.

The really good news is the amount of technological advances that have taken place in the past 20 years. When I began this journey, conducting this research was much more difficult. I had a computer. By then, most of us did. But we had just gotten a local phone number that enabled us to have dial-up Internet, and it was expensive. Think long-distance charges. And the World Wide Interweb, as Ron Burgundy calls it, was *slowww*. I once read an article in *PC Magazine* with the title "What Do You Do While Your Computer Boots Up?" Gives you an idea of how slow it really was. You could make a pot of coffee and clean up the dishes in the time it took to get ol' Dell up and running.

I had no cellphone or GPS. So I was often late for an appointment with a not-too-happy brewer because I couldn't call and let them know I'd gotten lost because of spotty directions and would be tardy. Hardly any of the microbreweries had websites. I think Shipyard and Gritty McDuff's had cursory ones, but not like today. There was no Trip Advisor or Yelp to tell you which place had great food and service or help you decide where to stay over if you were traveling to see breweries in a distant place. With Wi-Fi, a smartphone (it only took me five years to get one), a laptop, GPS, and Trip Advisor, my work is much easier.

I am still relying on what I called last time around "my Internet friends," people whom I met online, on home-brew digests mostly, who were kind enough to report back to me when they'd found a new brewpub or tasted a different beer. The difference now is that I'm meeting these people on Twitter, Facebook, and other social media. The other fantastic thing that I highly recommend you take advantage of are the beer bus tours that take you from brewery to brewery, sometimes including lunch, without your having to drive. Those are new on the scene, too. I've met fun, interesting people on these tours who are also really into tasting great beer.

So get ready for the ride on my own magic beer bus tour, an armchair tour. I'm bringing you my best effort at wrangling the brewers and owners and chefs and bartenders to give you a taste of what's brewing in New England.

WHAT IS A CRAFT BREWERY?

Your first resource for all things beer should be the Brewers Association (www.brewersassociation.org). Begun in the 1970s by Charlie Papazian, author of one of the bibles of home brewing, the association maintains a website that is the mother lode of statistics and other information, including the following definition of exactly what composes an American craft brewer (from the Brewers Association's Craft Beer website, www. craftbeer.com):

> An American craft brewer is small, independent and traditional.
>   Small: Annual production of 6 million barrels of beer or less.
>   Independent: Less than 25 percent of the craft brewery is owned or controlled (or equivalent economic interest) by an alcoholic beverage industry member that is not itself a craft brewer.
>   Traditional: A brewer that has a majority of its total beverage alcohol volume in beers whose flavor derives from traditional or innovative brewing ingredients and their fermentation. Flavored malt beverages (FMBs) are not considered beers.

Thanks to Andy Sparhawk and Bart Watson of the Brewers Association who responded to my many questions during the writing of this book.

How Beer Is Made on a Peter Austin System

By Mike Haley, Head Brewer at Kennebunkport Brewing Company, Kennebunkport, Maine

WE BREW SEVEN-BARREL BATCHES OF ENGLISH-STYLE ALES ON A TRA-ditional Peter Austin open-fermentation brewing system to supply the taps upstairs at our pub, Federal Jack's. We also function as a "production scale" pilot system for new product releases in the Shipyard family.

My favorite brew changes daily, depending on the weather, who is standing next to me, and how many hours I've spent in rubber boots, but my "go to" beers in the pub are the classic, balanced British Pale Ale, Taint Town Pale, and the flavorful, roasted, dark-chocolaty, herbal, soft and smooth Bluefin Stout.

At Kennebunkport Brewing Company (KBC) we use four main ingredients to produce our English-style ales, brewed on a traditional seven-barrel Peter Austin system, modeled after the famous Ringwood Brewery of Hampshire, England. The first is **filtered water.** All water used in the brewing process is first run through a carbon filter to remove chlorine and other compounds, then treated with brewing salts and phosphoric acid to achieve a consistent pH (usually around 5.0). This contributes to certain flavors and textures in the finished product as well as ensuring that we are starting with the same consistent base for each batch. In British brewing terms any water used in the brewing process is referred to as **liquor.** Because of this we refer to our hot water tank (the middle vessel in the brew-house) as the **hot liquor back,** or HLB.

Our second main ingredient is **malted barley.** All of our grains are imported from England and come to us having undergone the malting process. Malting is a four-step process in which the barley is soaked in water and is allowed to start germinating until the enzymes needed to convert starch to sugar are formed. When proper modification is achieved, the malt is then dried in a **kiln,** or drum-roasted, to develop specific color and flavor characteristics. Simply stated, we'll get the sugar that the yeast will need to produce alcohol later in our process, color will be determined by the types and amounts of specialty malts used, and the flavors of sweet, bready, caramel, chocolate, coffee, etc., will be contributed in varying levels depending on the beer style.

Our first step in the brewing process is to crack open each barley kernel, exposing the starches to the hot water. This allows for the conversion from starch to fermentable sugar. We do this by running all of the grain (on average, about 300 pounds) through our **grist mill,** the red machine in the mill room. After passing through the two-roller mill, the grain travels up the silver tube, the **auger,** and mixes together with 165-degree water from the hot liquor back in the **mash-tun,** which is the shorter vessel in the right corner of the brewhouse. This process is known as **mashing-in.**

We let this mixture of the malted barley and water sit in the mash-tun for 90 minutes, allowing for the enzymatic conversion of starches to fermentable sugars. Then we will "set taps," drawing this sugary-grain water, called **wort,** through the false bottom of the mash-tun, and over to the brick-clad **copper** or **brew kettle.** During the runoff, we will sparge hot brewing liquor, from the HLB, over the top of the mash bed to rinse all of the sugars from the malt.

It takes about two hours to run off all of the wort (about 210 gallons) from the mash-tun to the kettle, and shortly after our volume is reached, we will boil for one hour using three gas-fired burners under the kettle. During the runoff, and boil, we also have a whirling pump inside the kettle to promote even heating and prevent scorching the wort. The spent grains that are left behind in the mash-tun after the runoff are bagged for a local farmer to use as goat and pig feed.

It is at this time that we will add our third ingredient, **hops,** to the boiling wort. The hops we use are grown primarily in the Pacific Northwest US, but we do also use several British hop varieties, for their earthy, robust character befitting our most traditional of British beer styles.

Hops will contribute bitterness to balance the malt sweetness from the barley, and the delicate aromas that rise from the glass noticed before the first sip is taken. The hop cooler is like the brewer's spice rack, with different varieties contributing flavor and aroma descriptors of citrus, pine, herbal, spicy, grassy, earthy, floral . . .

After the boil, we let the wort continue to whirl for an additional hour, allowing any hop and/or grain solids that did not dissolve to settle out to the bottom of the kettle, before transferring the wort from the kettle and into the **fermentor.** But, before the wort enters the **fermentation vessel** (FV), we will first pass it through the **hop percolator** (HP), where we have been steeping 180-degree **hop tea,** made of the whole flower hops. This is where the majority of our hop aroma will come from.

The wort is then passed through the **heat exchanger.** The heat exchanger works the same way as a radiator. There are two separate channels in the series of metal plates: one for cold water and one for hot wort. The cold water will cool the wort to 68 to70 degrees F and the wort will continue on into the FV. The water is warmed by the wort and sent back into the HLB so we'll have hot water for the next day's brew. With the wort now at 68 degrees F, we are able to add our fourth main ingredient, **yeast**!

Our yeast is perhaps the most important ingredient in the entire process. The yeast that we use at KBC is known as "The Ringwood Yeast," so named for its origin at the Ringwood Brewery of Hampshire, England. This strain of ale yeast is over 150 years old, and was brought over from England by Master Brewer Alan Pugsley.

We begin with five pounds of yeast pitched directly into our traditional open-topped fermentation vessels. As the yeast ferments, it digests the sugar in the wort, producing alcohol and giving off CO_2 as byproducts. The CO_2 creates a protective layer over the top of the fermenting vessel to keep outside contaminants from entering the beer. The yeast will also reproduce itself, allowing us to re-pitch yeast from an active fermentation into a new batch. (That is how a yeast strain gets to be 150 years old!) The yeast will ferment actively, at temperatures between 68 and 70 degrees F, for three days until we've produced the desired amount of alcohol for that particular brand. We will then remove all but a thin layer of yeast from the top, and chill the beer to 40 degrees F by running our glycol coolant through coils inside the FV. The beer will remain in the FV for an additional three days (six days total), allowing the subtle flavors to develop and any dead yeast cells to drop to the bottom.

On day six, following the brew-day, we will **rack** the beer from the FV to our **conditioning tanks** (CTs). Here we will add two clarifying agents: isinglass, to remove yeast from suspension, and silica, to remove proteins. The beer remains in this tank for 24 hours at a temperature of 35 degrees F.

On day seven following the brew-day, we will **cold filter** the beer. We do this by running the beer through another heat exchanger (using glycol coolant instead of water, to get the beer colder), chilling the beer to 29 to 30 degrees F. This will cause any proteins and/or yeast still in the beer after conditioning to form a **chill haze.** Then we'll pump the beer through our **plate-and-frame-filter,** which will catch the yeast and proteins and leave us with bright, clear beer to fill our **serving** or **bright tanks** (in the cooler). We can then add CO_2 through a ceramic carbonating stone, producing fine bubbles that will stay in the beer. Finally, we will attach draft lines to the bottom of the serving tanks and push it directly upstairs to the faucets at Federal Jacks Restaurant and Brewpub.

Mike Haley is a lifelong Mainer with a degree from Springfield College. He began brewing at Shipyard Brewing Company in 1995, then moved to Kennebunkport Brewing Company as Head Brewer in 1998.

How to Use *What's Brewing in New England*

THIS IS PRIMARILY A TRAVEL GUIDE FOR WHAT PEOPLE ARE NOW CALLing "beer tourism." It's a listing of craft breweries and brewpubs that were in business or in the planning stages during the time I was writing this book. Here's how I found them:

- Brewers Association (www.brewersassociation.org): I perused their lists, and you can, too. Click on the Find a Brewery toggle on the website. I also interviewed Bart Watson, their staff economist.

- Twitter: I began following New England craft breweries, brewpubs, beer bars, bloggers, tourism magazines, and newspapers.

- Facebook: I am active on Facebook and posted daily or at least every few days about my progress on the book, asking (okay, pleading) for Facebook friends to write to me about their craft beer experiences. If you "like" my page, What's Brewing in Maine, you'll see my updates to the book once it comes out. And it will link to my blog, What's Brewing in Maine (www.whatsbrewing .bangordailynews.com).

- Beer bloggers: There are a lot of us! I signed up to get their newsletters and read their posts, often asking them to contribute their two cents to the book. Some of them agreed (joy!).

- Beer bus tours: I reached out to the beer bus operators and took a few tours to meet new brewers in other states, then I kept in touch with those people.

Listings: The breweries and brewpubs are listed alphabetically, by state, for expediency's sake. I included all of the information available to me. For instance, some breweries don't want to list a phone number, usually because they don't have a land line and don't want to use their cellphones for business. If a listing is missing a phone number, it isn't a mistake. The same is true of a website. Many small brewers use social media exclusively to publicize and update their clientele on new beers, adjusted hours, maybe even a new baby!

Call or visit the establishment's website or Facebook page for up-to-date information. Hours, tour availability, featured beers, etc., are constantly changing, so it's always a good idea to check before visiting.

What this book is and what it isn't: Well, of course I want everyone to read this guide and spread the word about how great it is. But frankly, and I say this with all due respect, I intended this book for people who love craft beer and like to travel around to try new breweries, but who may not themselves be brewers, certified beer judges, Cicerone-certified, or even home brewers. It's for the people on the beer bus tour, who like good food as much as they like the beer. It's for people who love the liquid in the glass, but may not know an ABV from an IBU and may never know or even care. They know "hoppy," and some like that, but they may stare off into space when the conversation starts going like this: "We dry hop with six different varieties like Cascade, Willamette . . ."

The book is *not* intended to be a review of the beers mentioned or the food served. There are any number of applications like Yelp, Trip Advisor, Urban Spoon, Beer Advocate, and Untappd to help readers hone their lists of places they want to visit and where to invest their time and money imbibing and noshing.

Length of brewery descriptions: This is a compilation of places to visit, and some got bigger write-ups than others. That is not intended to be my playing favorites. Not at all. I merely had some brewers/owners who were more available than others. Plain and simple. It was all about who could or would talk to me or had a person in their organization whose job it was to give out information. I am a big fan of craft brewers and hope they all succeed.

That was then, this is now: Where you see "That was then," it means I have taken the text from the first edition of *What's Brewing in New England* and placed it in this edition. Why? Because a lot of those pieces contain stories about the brewers or breweries that are still not only relevant, but give a rich snapshot of them from long ago. Where you see "This is now," it means I'm bringing you back to the present and letting you know what's going on at the time I did the interview or visited the brewery.

In their words: "In their words" means that I am quoting the brewer(s) or owner(s) from their Facebook page or website. I did this when I couldn't get anyone to return my phone calls or e-mails, and although I would much rather have had a personal interview, I made a decision to quote from those sources so readers would get more than just a name, address, and phone number listing.

Contact me: I would love to hear from you! Here's how to reach me:

Twitter: @kateconewrites

E-mail: kateconewrites@gmail.com

Facebook: www.facebook.com/What's Brewing in Maine. This is where I will be updating this book, so please come on over and "like" the page.

Blog: www.whatsbrewing.bangordailynews.com

Connecticut

My connection to the Nutmeg State goes back to the early 1600s. No, I'm not that old. My ancestor Daniel Cone, born in Edinburgh, came over from England with his wife, Mehitabel Spencer. I'm not only proud to be a descendant of one of the founders of Haddam, Connecticut, but also to be a relative of the Spencers, as in Lady Diana. No wonder I always had a tiara fantasy.

I recommend becoming a member of CT Beer Trail for Connecticut craft beer information. It's free and you can post or ask questions of the other members. If you tweet about beer in this state, use the hashtag #ctbeer, and you'll get quick responses from people who know the scene there. Bryon Turner, owner of CT Beer Trail, also gives bus tours. Lots of fun.

Back East Brewing
1296 Blue Hills Avenue, Suite A
Bloomfield, CT 06002-5312
(860) 242-1793
www.backeastbrewing.com

Opened in 2012 by Tony Karlowicz and Ed Fabricki, Tony gave me their story on a late summer day: "We began brewing in 2006 on a 10-gallon system, and by 2012 we were where we needed to be. It took six months to move the equipment in and we sold our first beer in July 2012, our golden ale. We wanted to do something really simple for our first batch. Ed's an engineer and I have a business background, so we have a good balance with where our skills and interests are. Ed is Mr. Inside, handling production, and I'm Mr. Outside, running the business.

"We took the building next door to us, doubling our size and doubling production. We have a small tasting room that's open Wednesday through Saturday. We have a manufacturer's permit where you can give tours and samples. We're proud of the fact that we have a really good lineup of beers—none of them is on the chopping block. Our porter has won three medals, including one at the American Craft Beer Awards. We were the second brewery in Connecticut to can all of our beers. Our most popular beers lately are Palate Mallet and our Summer Ale, both very hoppy with West Coast hops."

When I asked Tony for a recommendation for a local eatery, he suggested Republic and Carbone's Kitchen, both in Bloomfield.

Beer'd Brewing Company

22 Bayview Avenue, #15
Stonington, CT 06378-1014
(860) 857-1014
www.beerdbrewing.com

Eric Ciocca has traveled all over New England to taste craft beer. One of his favorite breweries is Beer'd in Stonington, as this thoughtful piece, "Stonington on My Mind," shows:

> *The borough of Stonington is like an island lost in time. It is divided from the rest of town by railroad tracks, only accessible by a curiously complex overpass. As you crest this bridge it seems to rewind the years—on one side is a typical southern Connecticut town, the other is a densely packed New England village of sturdily built stone buildings and automobile-unfriendly streets. The history practically oozes from every inn and church. Tall ships are frequently visible from Stonington Point, on their way to or from nearby Mystic.*
>
> *Just slightly inland (nearby on the "modern" side of the bridge) is The Velvet Mill. Repurposed from its original textile production, the mill now houses space for artists, craftsmen, bakers, and a Saturday*

farmers' market. Deep in the labyrinth of industrial corridors and studios, behind an immense sliding metal door adorned with a giant beard, is the nano-sized Beer'd Brewing. This brewery, although small in stature, has quickly grown to become a local darling that supplies regularly returning customers with their weekend's brews one growler at a time. Beer'd can occasionally be found on tap in local bars (of note, The Engine Room in Mystic), but it focuses on providing beer directly to the people. This makes production a constant balancing act between making enough staple beers to provide for the upcoming weekend and making a few quickly disappearing experimental batches.

Beer'd's flagship is their Whisker'd Wit (5.2% ABV), a citrusy and yeasty Belgian-style wit that goes equally as well with a summer day as a heavy meal. Visitors to the brewery are afforded liberal samples while they choose their favorite, but even a briskly decided visitor should take the time to enjoy a little "wit while [you] wait."

Beer'd's artistic strength is in their IPAs. Brewer Aaren Simoncini offers interesting combinations of hops from around the world in rotating availability. Lovers of Kiwi hops will like the yeasty and dry Vegemite Sandwich (9.5% ABV) and the fruity Hobbit Juice (9.2% ABV). The Grove Stand (9.2% ABV) provides an American-style Citra hit. But the can't-miss beer here is the Dogs and Boats (9.1% ABV), a thick, juicy, and thirst-quenching wall of flavor. For the faint-of-hops its baby-cousin APA, Kittens and Canoes (5.7% ABV), provides a slightly less intense but no less enjoyable flavor.

Growler laws in Connecticut allow you to fill glass from any brewery, so you can bring your favorite or buy a fresh growler. If you hit the brewery on the day of a farmers' market, you can buy a snack and enjoy a small picnic in the mill or on the nearby beach. Hard to find but easy to drink, Beer'd goes by a motto stenciled on their brewery wall: They're not trying to stand out in a crowd, but stand on their own somewhere else.

Eric Ciocca is a programmer, runner, and beer-traveler from Northampton, MA. His superpowers involve being everywhere at once and always finding just the right beer for the occasion. He also draws a web comic about nothing in particular: www.paranoiddreams.com.

Black Pond Brews
21 Furnace Street
Danielson, CT 06239
(860) 208-6829
www.blackpondbrews.com

Mike Teed and Cory Smith started brewing in 2010 and four short years later opened Black Pond. I'm sure those four years didn't seem short, given the licensing hoops most brewers have to jump through, but you can now visit and get growler fills of Razor Blades IPA, Israel Putnam Brown Ale, CT Uncommon Lager, and Machu Picchu Jalapeño Saison. The website is kept up to date on the beers they have available each week.

I got my answer to "Do you give tours?" via text message: "We are a tiny, one room brewery, so the tour is effectively over once you come in!" There you have it.

Brewery Legitimus
283 Main Street
New Hartford, CT 06057
www.brewerylegitimus.com

"Legitimus IPA will be one of the first beers out of the gate when we open, if all goes as planned," owner Chris Sayer told me. With the voices of sweet-sounding kiddos in the background, he and I chatted about the "crazy" pace at which craft breweries are opening. "When I worked in the beer business in 2002," he said, "I could say I'd tried every craft beer in New England. Now, that's impossible." Legitimus will finish the "build-out" phase of its brewery construction process, which includes navigating the perilous waters of zoning approvals and other licensing procedures.

Chris caught the "beer bug" in Belgium, where he spent time during college, and worked in sales at Harpoon, then Duvel and Ommegang. But he isn't limiting himself to the Belgian and American styles he's thinking of brewing. Smart move! Check their website and Facebook page for opening news.

Broad Brook Brewing Company

2 North Road
East Windsor, CT 06088
(860) 623-1000
www.broadbrookbrewing.com

Opened in 2013 by Eric Mance and his two partners, Broad Brook has a spacious taproom that they "really put a lot into," according to Eric. He told me their most popular beer is Hopstillo IPA, which contains at least seven types of hops. Take a look at the virtual tour on their website. And free Wi-Fi? Well, then . . . One could just live there. They encourage a bring-your-own-food policy, but also offer a menu book of local eateries that deliver to the brewery.

In their words: "We were tired of drinking bland beer that fell flat on our taste buds. So in September 2010, we decided it was time to take matters into our own hands and we started to brew some of the finest beer in New England." Beers on tap include the year-round Broad Brook Ale, Porter's Porter, Hopstillo IPA, and Chet's Session IPA, along with seasonals such as 7th Heaven IPA, No BS Brown Ale, Oktoberfest, 6 Balls Alt, Dark Star IPA, Chocolate Oatmeal Stout, Homewrecker Holiday Ale, and Season of the Witch.

Brü Room At BAR

254 Crown Street
New Haven, CT 06511-6610
(203) 495-8924
www.barnightclub.com

That was then: Opened in 1996, Brü Room is located within a block of Yale University and caters to the casual crowd it attracts from the campus and environs. Decor is industrial: bare concrete walls mixed with exposed brickwork, conduits, and pipes. The menu features brick-oven-baked pizza and one salad.

This is now: One diner raved about the pizza, service, and beer in a *Beer Advocate* post in June 2014. Their menu is still "pizza forward" and they have a salad bar, along with live music and dancing. The interior is indeed somewhat industrial, with part of the brewery smack in the dining area, but it has lots of warm wood touches and booths that soften the metal.

There are four separate areas that have different "feels." For instance, the Front Room features an antique pool table and long beer garden tables and can be reserved for groups of 10 to 80 people. The Lounge is quieter and suits folks who might want more intimate conversation. Then there is the Bartropolis Dance Floor, where I suspect most of the action happens. Good idea, offering something to suit just about every taste. And congrats for their longevity.

Speaking of longevity, here is the brewer's description of one of their originals, Toasted Blonde: "This is the same Blonde that you've had for years, only now it's toasted . . . Nicely toasted. Notice that it has an enhanced biscuit toasty taste and a light, dry finish." The beer selection is varied and includes their own five or six house brews as well as many other breweries' beers.

Cambridge House Brew Pub

357 Salmon Brook Street
Granby, CT 06035-0478
(860) 653-2739
www.cbhgranby.com

Mike Yates took over the brewing duties in the summer of 2015 and is keeping the flagship Abija Rowe IPA and award-winning Copper Hill Kolsch on tap all the time, while rotating other brews through the lineup. Check out the blog at their website for some in-depth writing about their different beers, how they're made, and why they're special.

Although it seems from the menu that the food is bar/pub fare, they are tweaking it to accommodate vegans, vegetarians, lactose-intolerant, gluten-free, and even Paleo eaters. Take a look at the description of one of their salads, Paleo-friendly and looking delicious (check out their Facebook photos): "Apple Pecan Bleu Cheese Salad in Belgian Endive spoons topped with crispy prosciutto & orange honey vinaigrette." Then you have your pizza, sandwiches and wraps, burgers, a few salads, and the kind of appetizers you'd expect: onion rings, nachos, calamari. If those are done impeccably, they're all you need.

City Steam Brewery Café
942 Main Street
Hartford, CT 06103-1214
(860) 525-8213
www.citysteam.biz

It was an unseasonably sunny and warm March day when my husband and I took a ride with Bryon Turner on CT Beer Trail's brewery bus tour. Happy to get out of the frigid Maine never-ending winter weather, we had driven down the night before and stayed with my son Burke, who had just begun a job at Dean College. I had a case of nerves, since I was the featured guest on this tour (who me?), but Bryon had arranged for another special guest to be aboard the bus: someone whose identity he didn't reveal until an hour or so into the schedule. Ron Page, longtime brewmaster at City Steam, stealthily infiltrated our pack of drinkers, then hosted us at his workplace.

Although we had lunch in a private room, we had plenty of time to wander around this historic building smack in the center of downtown Hartford. Originally home to a seven-level late 19th-century department store (think Selfridges, if you're a PBS-TV fan), this brewpub sprawls yet feels homey, with wood-paneled rooms that evoke bars and restaurants of a bygone era.

Head brewer Ron Page came along on our epic tour of six craft breweries that day, and I managed to get him to answer some questions on a busy brew day.

Kate: How long have you been brewing, and could you name the breweries?

Ron: I started brewing professionally in 1990, at age 36, at the New England Brewing Company, in Norwalk, Connecticut, along with Phil Markowski [Markowski is now owner/brewer at Two Roads]. At the time there were approximately 100 breweries in the whole country. I moved to Elm City, aka New Haven Brewing Company, in 1994 and have been working at City Steam since 1997.

K: You said in an interview with *Writer's Bone* that you began home brewing because you ran out of beer on a Sunday. Could you tell readers that story, since many of them, especially the millennials, wouldn't know about blue laws?

R: Ah, the bad old days. Connecticut was the second to last state in the Union to prohibit Sunday sales of alcohol. . . . However, like any illegal substance, the calendar held little actual sway if one knew where to look . . . bodegas in Willimantic, pharmacies in New Haven, some old guy's garage in Hartford, etc., etc. My real reason for home brewing, economics aside, was to be able to try to make the kind of beers you could only dream about from reading [Michael] Jackson's *World Guide to Beer.*

K: What inspires the names behind the beers? Where did Naughty Nurse come from, for instance?

R: Most beer names come to me while riding to work on I-91, listening to music, on the day of the brew. Silly sexual suggestions aside, I believe that of all the arts, brewers come closest to musicians in practicing an ever-evolving, sensual form of expression. Beer labels are like song titles. Too bad we can't collect royalties!

K: What's your beer palate like after all these years? Do you like a few particular styles, or do you try everything?

R: Actually, being of distant French heritage, I mostly drink wine when I'm not being paid to drink beer. If I had to pick a favorite type of beer, it would be the clean, malty flavors of European lagers. I don't take beer as seriously as some others, and consider drinking good beer a pleasant and relaxing way to pass the time, not something to be studied and agonized over.

K: Tell me about your reserve beers . . . I think you mentioned to me on our tour that the photos you use on the posters were considered porn at one time? Could you elaborate on what you're going for with those?

R: The old-fashioned "porn" labels are really just images taken from old turn-of-the-last-century "French postcards." I guess I was trying to show that there is really nothing new under the sun, as far as the concept of young women and beer drinking as a natural wonder. What distinguishes the labels further, however, is the original verse that accompanies each image. I've been told not to quit my day job in the pursuit of literary heights.

K: When you're kicking back at home, what's a likely dinner either cooked with beer or paired with beer?

R: Cooking was my first love and is something I do every day, from baking bread to smoking meats to making sausage and preserving fruits and vegetables. I like to drink beer with salty or greasy food, and rarely use it in the dish itself, as the hops tend to alter the flavor in a negative way. I much prefer using wine or spirits in a dish. That being said, last night I made spareribs, sauerkraut, and new potatoes braised in Export lager.

K: At the brewpub, do you take suggestions from customers when deciding what types of beer to brew?

R: Sometimes they pay me to make a beer in their honor.

K: I won't ask you what beer you'd take on a desert island, so I'll ask what beer did you drink before craft beer became so readily available? [I drank Heineken and Beck's after I graduated from Miller Lite.]

R: Interesting question. In the 1970s, when I was seriously learning how to drink beer, we could occasionally find Ballantine India Pale Ale, along with Bass Ale, John Courage, Sam Smith's Pale Ale, Heineken Dark, Spaten Wheat, German Löwenbräu, even Ringnes Bock from Norway. My first taste of Anchor Liberty Ale was almost a religious experience.

K: What are three things you think are big changes in the craft beer industry in New England in the time you've been brewing?

R: I don't think much has really changed in terms of the dedication, ingenuity, and creativity of the brewers. The customers, however, are more aware of difference in beer styles and are willing to experiment. Obviously, one factor is the proliferation of small breweries. I predict someday there may be one in every town, just like local pizzerias. Modern brewers also have a distinct advantage in the incredible availability of different forms of raw material, i.e., unique hop, malt, and yeast varieties that were unheard of even 10 years ago.

K: Have any of the beer law changes affected City Steam in any significant way? For instance, is the proliferation of brewers selling directly to customers in tasting rooms affecting the brewpub business?

R: If I was 10 years younger, and not so close to retirement [Ron retired in March 2016], I would probably try to start a nanobrewery myself. As romantic and enticing as such a venture may seem— especially through the fog of a couple dozen home brews—brewing is and always will be a business first. . . . If you can't sell enough beer to pay your costs and make a living, then the brewery will close.

Ron gave me a poster that day showing a scantily clad 19th-century woman sitting on a gent's lap, the pair outlined by a large keyhole:

Mr. Page's Private Reserve: Special Ale Number One

CURIOSITY:
Peeking through a keyhole can sometimes cause a shock
Some people do it all the time—others will wisely balk
At the risk of seeing something they should never see . . .
If any of this makes any sense, well, you've drank more ale than me!
Verse by Ron Page

Cottrell Brewing Company

100 Mechanic Street
Pawcatuck, CT 06379-2163
(860) 599-8213
www.cottrellbrewing.com

Owner and brewer Charlie Buffam was studying in London when he began his journey with great beers and ales. On his return to Connecticut, he quit his day job and began brewing, the dream of many a day-job-holding would-be brewer. On February 28, 1997, Charlie and his wife Ann "rolled the first keg of Old Yankee Ale down Mechanic Street to our local watering hole, C.C. O'Brien's." Charlie is the great-great grandson of C. B. Cottrell, the owner of a company that manufactured printing presses, and he's proud to continue the Cottrell legacy of owning a local business making a local product.

Cottrell Brewing's flagship Old Yankee Ale (5% ABV), brewed since 1997, is described as "a medium-bodied, American amber ale that has a great up-front malt taste with a refreshing hop finish," making it an outstanding session beer for any occasion. If you visit in person, you can taste one of a number of "nano-brews," experimental beers the team plays with that are served only in the tasting room.

DuVig Brewery

59 School Ground Road, Unit #10
Branford, CT 06405
(203) 208-2213
www.duvig.com

Catching someone on a Saturday, when they are trying to be nice to the visitors and not snarl at some unknown person (me) who's interrupting them, is difficult. But Colin, the assistant brewer, did just that on a wearily awful-weather day in December. When asked if they give tours, Colin said, "You show up, we will give a tour, which explains the process of making the beer, which is easy because it's a 7 bbl system. It's pretty simple. If it's a brew day, it's harder, but we try to accommodate."

Colin, the only employee besides the owners, says he "does all sorts of things when [he's] not brewing: work the front room, secretary, janitor, sales representative, and giver of information to the travel guide writer [me again]."

Living in New England inspires lots of things: There's Robert Frost and his poetry based on his years in New Hampshire, then there's Mark Twain, who lived in Connecticut and who said, "If you don't like the weather in New England now, just wait a few minutes." The blizzard of 2013 inspired the Dugas and Vigliotti families to start a brewery. Being trapped with their own home brews was a lightbulb moment, when they realized there weren't many options for high-quality beers as good as theirs.

When I visited, DuVig was about to release a Scottish-style ale, which will be their winter ale. According to Colin, "We have four beers available: three mainstays and a seasonal. We do growler fills, too, and flights of four for tastings. We'd love to begin canning the beer, but we'd like to own the canning line ourselves. We'll consider it in a year or so."

Firefly Hollow Brewing Company

139 Center Street, Suite 5005
Bristol, CT 06010-5086
(860) 845-8977
www.fireflyhollowbrewing.com

Yup, you guessed it: Firefly was a stop on our famous CT Beer Trail tour. It was a Saturday afternoon and that tasting room was *rocking*. People brought in their own food and a group was celebrating a birthday, bellied up to the bar or sitting at tables enjoying the beer. Brewer Dana Bourque stood above us in the brewery with goggles on. He looked like the firefly in their logo, except Dana would be hard-pressed to ever look menacing. He was the very image of Shakespeare's playful Puck, gleefully talking about his process and the fast success of the brewery and taproom.

This tour is where I met Frank and Bonnie Presto, the people I now think of as model beer lovers: He loves hops, she does not, yet they are a happily married couple who spend a lot of time touring and tasting beer. They told me that Firefly is one of their favorite taprooms to frequent. It is a must-see while in Connecticut.

Dana Bourque loves when returning customers tell him what beers they liked, so he can bring them back. So far, they've brewed over 25 types of beers, and there's always something interesting cooking up in the back of his noggin. Food trucks now come out to the brewery a few times a week, and there is also some live music.

Half Full Brewery

43 Homestead Avenue
Stamford, CT 06902-7204
(203) 658-3631
www.halffullbrewery.com

From Wall Street banker to full-time brewer . . . that's a career trajectory enviable for most people still stuck in their day jobs! But Conor Horrigan did it. The description of the flagship beer, Bright Ale (5.2% ABV), tells the story: "That bright idea. You know the type . . . Your mind races. Your stomach flutters. You feel alive. A confluence of events sparked my bright idea; beers one night in NYC, a life-changing trip, and a push from a friend all led to . . . 'I'll open a brewery!' Half Full Bright Ale, the perfect inspirational pairing for whenever you want to entertain that bright idea."

Charlotte was working the taproom when I called to find out more. She told me there is a $5 tasting with five samples, and customers get to keep the sample glass. For $15 you get a pint glass and open sampling. "We opened in 2012 and drastically increased distribution this past year [2014], expanding into New York," she said. "And we just purchased a few more fermenting tanks and a new canning line."

Hog River Brewing Company

1429 Park Street
Hartford, CT 06106
www.hogriverbrewingcompany.com

When Hog River Brewing Company was getting close to opening in 2016, they even invited fans into the brewery one evening via their

Facebook page for a sneak peek. Ben Braddock, formerly of Willimantic Brewing Company, is jumping into the brewing fray on his own at Hog River in the Parkville area of Hartford. Ben began his journey when "my cubicle walls started closing in on me." That corporate or professional noose has spurred many of the brewers I know to take a leap into a more creative endeavor like making beer.

Ben started out cleaning kegs (a noble and necessary task—sanitation is everything in this business), and at this writing was serving his beers at brewfests. Check Facebook and Twitter for updates.

Kent Falls Brewing Company
33 Camps Road
Kent, CT 06757
(860) 398-9645
www.kentfallsbrewing.com

Located on a 43-acre former dairy farm, Kent Falls Brewing brought back the property to its original function by establishing itself as a "farmhouse" brewery. Growing or sourcing ingredients for its beer either on the farmland it occupies or getting it from others within a 50-mile radius, Barry Labendz and his partners are practicing true sustainability. The beers? To start, they are making a saison and a porter.

In their words: "As a farmhouse brewery, we aim to make unique beers that are a product of our land and environment: water from our own wells, hops from our own yard, and yeast harvested from the air flowing around our property (not to mention off apple skins and other fruit around the farm)."

When I spoke with Barry, he told me "Kent Falls is in the final construction phase of the brewery. It was more cost effective to build a new rather than reconstruct the old dairy barn. The barn will be a barrel-aging facility." Regarding their status as a "farmhouse brewery," Barry said, "The state does not have ties between brewing and agriculture. The town of Kent worked with us to create the farmhouse brewery permit. Our goal is not to grow everything that goes into the beer, but if we want to make a pumpkin or squash beer, we know local farmers who do grow them. It's such a nice network of people, we love being able to support a wider network of farms."

Kent Falls won't have tastings and tours out of the starting gate. Barry explains, "Part of the zoning regulations involve a secondary permit for tours and tastings. In the future, we want to apply for that permit. But the hop farm and apple orchard are open to the public." For now, they'll place their beers, "in any place that focuses on good food and beer. Litchfield County will be our focus so we can serve our local community. But we'll be distributing in eastern Connecticut eventually."

Derek Dellinger, a longtime home brewer whose articles about beer have been published in various beer periodicals, will create the beers. Follow their progress on their website and on Facebook.

New England Brewing Company
175 Amity Street
Woodbridge, CT 06525-2217
(203) 387-2222
www.newenglandbrewing.com

NEBC makes memorable beers like Fuzzy Baby Ducks and Imperial Stout Trooper, but the one that was over-the-top popular was their Gandhi Bot IPA. In 2015, after a lawsuit was filed in India claiming that the name and logo of a robotic Mahatma Gandhi dishonored the memory of the Indian hero and peace activist, NEBC decided to change the name. It's the same beer, but now called G-Bot. While writing this book, I heard so much about this IPA, almost as much as The Alchemist's Heady Topper, that I thought it alone must be worth a trip to Connecticut. NEBC describes the beer as an intensely hopped double IPA with a blend of three varieties of American hops. Distributed only in the Nutmeg State, you'll have to get there yourself to taste it.

Check their Facebook page and Twitter feed for events and happenings, like yoga at the brewery!

No Worries Brewing Company

2520 State Street
Hamden, CT 06517
(203) 691-6662
www.noworriesbeer.com

From dream to reality . . . No Worries was open and showing March Madness on their taproom tellies when I stopped by one day. People love the beer, and how can you argue with a brewery that stays open until the UConn Huskies finish their basketball game? Burning the midnight oil for a good cause, i.e., local sports teams.

Dan Whittle and Kevin Mark are finally brewing. The most recent beers getting raves are their flagship Good Ryebrations, a rye pale ale offering a distinct bite from rye malt balanced with caramel malt and citrusy hops, and Satisfaction DIPA, boasting a blend of US, New Zealand, and Australian hops and an 8.2% ABV. Food is supplied by local food trucks, including the Spud Stud: Gourmet baked potatoes, burgers, hot dogs, wraps, "and so much more" go just fine with No Worries' thirst-slaking beers.

Noble Jay Brewing Company

11 Freedom Way
Niantic, CT 06357
www.noblejaybrew.com

Mike Lincoln, a University of Maine graduate, told me that "the permitting process takes a long time," and Noble Jay, named in a roundabout way for his late mother, was still planning to open as this book went to press. But they have their brewery site and will welcome beer lovers to their taproom with some flagship brews like Mo Pilsner, a pre-Prohibition-style pilsner, and Fatty Boom Boom, a lagered Baltic porter, among many others. "We feel craft lagers are underrepresented in Connecticut and can't wait to turn people on to the smooth and sultry nature of these slow, cold, and bottom-fermented craft brews," Mike said. A recreation and tourism major, he will have no trouble getting people to make the trek to try his beers and take a tour.

OEC Brewing

7 Fox Hollow Road
Oxford, CT 06478-3162
(203) 295-2831
www.oecbrewing.com

Good thing they decided to call their company OEC, because here's what it stands for, in their words: *Ordinem Ecentrici Coctores = Order of the Eccentric Boilers.* They go on to say that they are poking fun at the secret societies of old. Well, there's something in the air, or water, or any other of the five elements, because in less than a year, OEC has turned out over 21 styles of beer. Their beer list will make you dizzy.

OEC's Facebook page is up to date, announcing their newest beers, like this duo: Exilis, a Berliner-style Weisse, and Salsus (Blend #2), their interpretation of a rustic Gose. Their special tours sell out months in advance, so check the website and purchase tickets fast.

Olde Burnside Brewing Company

780 Tolland Street
East Hartford, CT 06108-2727
(860) 528-2200
www.oldeburnsidebrewing.com

The McClellan clan celebrated 15 years in business in early 2016. Bob, his wife Gail, and their sons Jason and Case keep the beers coming as the oldest family-owned microbrewery in the state. They even sponsor their own Celtic music festival, called Pipes in the Valley, each September. The festival attracts over 20,000 people to Hartford.

A unique water source and English malts help create these beers. In their words: "Using only the choicest ingredients coupled with our own unique pure water source located on our property, with similar mineral characteristics as the water in Burton-on-Trent, Olde Burnside Brewing handcrafts traditional ales with a Scottish twist."

The Ten Penny Ale (5.6% ABV) gets raves and is described as follows: "Our flagship Scottish Ale, malty with a hint of caramel and a hint of smokiness. Just enough hops to balance the malt. Very sessionable."

Outer Light Brewing Company

266 Bridge Street
Groton, CT 06340
(475) 201-9972
www.outerlightbrewing.com

When I first spoke with Tom Drejer, he explained the choice of his new brewery's name: "Outer Light is a nickname taken from the Saybrook Breakwater Lighthouse located at the mouth of the Connecticut River and serves as a mystical, gleaming light of hope at a journey's end for generations of sailors."

Tom and co-owner Matt Ferrucci met through a college friend, and both have been home brewing for years. At their new brewery in the submarine capital of the world, the pair share brewing fun with head brewer Tyler Cox. I managed to speak with Tom again right after he and Matt celebrated Outer Light's first anniversary. Their newest beer, Hoppy Beer Day DIPA, was followed soon afterward by Outer Weiss Hefeweizen.

Outer Light has a tasting room with growler fills, but doesn't serve food. Tom coordinates with the local food-truck scene for food options. If you want to visit the brewery and eat later, he recommends the Spot Cafe, Shack Restaurant, and Paul's Pasta Shop right in Groton.

Overshores Brewing Company

250 Bradley Street
East Haven, CT 06512
(206) 909-6224
www.overshores.com

The first brewery in Connecticut to dedicate itself solely to brewing the Belgian style, Overshores—opened in 2014—makes five bottle-conditioned brews and serves other companies' Belgians in their tasting room. Founder and CEO Christian Amport came out of the architecture business, where he designed Starbucks stores. "I appreciated working for a company that makes a premium product," he says. "They take coffee really seriously. People love it and it makes them happy. I decided I wanted to do the same for beer."

Powder Hollow

504 Hazard Avenue
Enfield, CT 06082
(860) 205-0942
www.powderhollowbrewery.com

The best part of writing a book like this is talking to brewers who were planning their breweries and learning that they have fulfilled their dreams. Mike McManus is one of many I can congratulate not only on opening, but celebrating that first-year anniversary.

The construction-engineer-turned-brewery-owner talked about his new place, which opened in 2014: "The brewery is located in an old industrial complex that made solar panels, and at one point, they did toy testing to see how durable they are. That part is our brewing pad. Visitors can come in and get a taste of the beer and growler fills. We have food trucks coming by, and people are welcome to bring their own food. We make a lot of IPAs, stouts, porters, all inspired by home brewing. I've been making some experimental batches, one with lime basil and one called Slightly Skewed, an IPA aged with cedar wood. The rotation will change all the time, and I'll have some that are always out there."

Mike says his most popular beers, of the 13 on tap, are West Coast Citrus IPA and Smoky Aftermath, which people call "the bacon beer." The Early Morning Oatmeal Stout is available only in the taproom, so turn on your GPS and get driving. Powder Hollow beers are now in over 250 locations, both restaurants and liquor stores, in Connecticut. Congrats and continued great luck!

Relic Brewing
95B Whiting Street
Plainville, CT 06062-2842
(860) 255-4252
www.relicbeer.com

Relic is a case in point of how each craft brewer has a different vision for his or her beers and where and how they present them to the adoring public. Yes, this was another stop on the CT Beer Trail Magical Mystery Tour. The tasting room here is small but cozy, and the day we barged in, the walls were covered in the works of a local artist. Gallery, brewery, tasting room . . . very nice. On tap back then was Biere de Noel (7.8% ABV), described as "dark, malty but balanced, hints of chocolate and clove," among many, many other creations. That spring they brewed a pale ale with Valencia oranges that was so popular, they brought it back the following year. Named Connecticut's best nanobrewery by *Food & Wine* magazine in 2014, Relic has distinguished itself nicely.

Shebeen Brewing Company
1 Wolcott Road
Wolcott, CT 06716-2611
(203) 514-2336
www.shebeenbrewing.com

This was our last stop on the CT Beer Trail Tour, and my bus mates showed no signs of slowing down. Mike Visco, head brewer, has an MBA from the University of Connecticut. He says, "I wrote my master's thesis on microbreweries. I wanted to open a brewery years ago, but Connecticut wasn't culturally ready." I got another level of that explanation from Tony Markowski at Two Roads: "This state has been corporate headquarters for many imported beers for decades. So it took a very long time for beer drinkers to switch not just from Budweiser or other big American beers, but from Heineken, St. Pauli Girl, Becks. Now they are on board."

Mike is living proof. His cannoli beer is hugely popular, and, yes, it tastes like cannoli. There are palates suited for that style of beer—mine likes things less sweet. But Mike brews something for everyone. In fact, he says he loves selling his beer out of his brewery because, "I love talking to people in my tasting room. They give me feedback, and I can brew a beer they want the next week."

Southport Brewing Company and Restaurant
2600 Post Road
Southport, CT 06890-1258
(203) 256-2337
www.southportbrewing.com

Since 1997 Southport Brewing has been offering full menus and now 27 different beers. They announced a new beer in what they are calling their Hydroponic series, described as follows: "Hydroponic Session has the same great flavors of the white with a hefty dry hop of citra hops giving Hydro Session tons of orange and tropical fruit flavor!" The SBC Facebook page is up to date with brewer's notes about what they're brewing and experimenting with.

Check their website for more locations, as well as specials, happy hours, karaoke nights, and other events. Not only do they feed you here, but Southport also caters. I wonder if Connecticut will ever allow beer delivery? They're doing it in Boston, folks!

The food menu has just about anything you could want, from stout onion soup to Australian sea bass, truffle mac and cheese, pizza, and salads. Reviews appear to be mixed, from excellent to not so. But having been in the restaurant business, I know two things: Stuff happens, and you really need to be consistently excellent.

Steady Habit Brewing Company
95 Bridge Road
Haddam, CT 06438
(860) 316-8987
www.steadyhabitbrewing.com

Jon Peterson and Kirk Fontaine opened Steady Habit on January 17, 2015. Jon explained the name Steady Habit: "Back in the 1800s,

Connecticut earned the nickname 'The Land Of Steady Habits.' The core of the nickname implied wise governance, stability and virtue."

With Jon doing the brewing and Kirk running the business, the pair offers several beers. The flagship is Our Daily Bread, an IPA with 6% ABV and 60 IBUs, but Jon had many more planned at the time of opening: "We're open one or two days a week for growler fills, to take beer to go, and we'll let people sample beforehand. Eventually we'll get the license to sell pints and have food trucks come around."

Jon began brewing a decade ago and gradually became drawn to the idea of opening his own brewery. "I'm constantly tweaking recipes," he says. "I love to make hoppy IPAs that are not too bitter. I was always thinking of taking my brewing to the next level." They prefer you check their Facebook page for news and updates.

Make filling your growlers a steady habit (sorry), then head across the historic swing bridge to East Haddam, where you can grab lunch or dinner at the Gelston House, a gastropub with "good food and multiple taps," according to Jon. His favorite place for pizza is La Vita Gustosa, an authentic Italian trattoria that was advertising an upcoming four-course beer dinner, convenient for that Saturday evening when you can stay over afterwards.

Stony Creek Brewery
5 Indian Neck Road
Branford, CT 06405
www.stonycreekbeer.com

Stony Creek Brewery opened in 2012 in Stony Creek, Connecticut, and it didn't take them long to expand to a much bigger facility. The spectacular new brewery is now open on the banks of the Branford River and attracting over 1,500 people on a Saturday afternoon, according to director of operations Manny Rodriguez. At nearly 30,000 square feet, it features two outdoor decks, a tasting room, and a celebration room, all designed by Branford architect Joe Sepot.

Their "aggressively laid back beers" are now available in Connecticut, Rhode Island, and Massachusetts in cans, bottles, and on draft. Included in the lineup are those in the "cranky" series: Cranky IPA (6.8% ABV), Big Cranky Double IPA (9.5% ABV), and Little Cranky Session IPA (4.5% ABV). The brewer's description of Big Cranky goes like this: "A Bold West Coast Double IPA, this is the crankiest of our IPAs. Seven different hops contribute complex and juicy hop character. Its dry finish allows the hops to stand out. At 9.5% ABV and 95 IBUs, while remarkably cranky, this beer is extraordinarily drinkable." Manny invites folks to bring a picnic or enjoy food from one of the local food trucks that visit the brewery.

Stubborn Beauty

180 Johnson Street
Middletown, CT 04657
www.stubbornbeauty.com

This brewery was brand spanking new the week we made it our first stop on the CT Beer Trail tour. Sampling beer at 10:30 in the morning seemed a little weird at first, but when in Rome, as they say.

Owner Shane Lentini and I did a little Q&A via e-mail to catch up since they opened:

Kate: Have you finally gotten your bigger brewing equipment? You were waiting for it back then.

Shane: Yes! The equipment literally rolled in on the truck on Easter Sunday [2014] . . . not a bad way to spend Easter getting to unload and set up your new brewhouse and tanks!

K: Tell me about opening night. How many people showed up? And you ran out of beer?

S: We were running out of beer the first month or two! It was crazy but we expected it to happen. We were still brewing on our tiny 1 bbl brewhouse . . . and even all the crazy brewing we did months prior in anticipation of not having enough proved to be rather futile. We actually had to close a couple Saturdays over the first couple of months so we could "catch up" on brewing. Now doing 7 bbl at a time, this hasn't (yet) become an issue. Plenty of beer is flowing from the tasting room—we regularly have six to eight beers on tap and our distribution network is growing every week. We are actually just about to sign on with G&G Beverage Distributors to get our product to New Haven and Fairfield Counties! There just aren't enough hours in the day to self-distribute to those counties.

K: How are things now? Have you added more beers?

S: We are always adding more and/or new beers. I don't remember what or how many beers we had on tap when you came by . . . but we're on a pretty solid rotation where our "staples" (I use that term loosely) are in a somewhat constant rotation. In between we stick to our eclectic roots and create new beasts. We released our first Sour (an Oud Bruin) about a month ago, and the feedback has been stellar. We are also in the final stages of doing our first "brewery only" bottle release—our 14% imperial stout will be limited to approximately 150 16-ounce bottles sold directly from the brewery. ETA is October for the release.

K: Any changes planned for the near future?

S: To continue with the beer garden/patio, we are also going to be expanding our Connecticut permit to allow us to be able to sell pints directly from the brewery. This is something we really weren't interested in out of the gate. But as with any business, you have to be able to step back and take a look at the landscape and, well, sometimes that means your opinions change. However, we still don't plan on having "bar type hours" or anything of the sort. It's just another nice option for our customers to be able to grab a full beer, sit outside, and enjoy it.

Tidal River Brewing Company
15 Cheryl Drive
Canton, CT 06019
(860) 386-8033
www.tidalriverbrewing.com

This brewery was in the planning stages when I first contacted its owner. Geoff Mattheis was so engaging, I am including the interview here, in his words: "I'm a single operator LLC. I'll be handling the business and the brewing myself with lots of volunteer help! My brewing background is strictly amateur. I've been home brewing for about three years now, built up a decent cache of recipes and experience. I really like to branch out, challenge myself, and try new stuff all the time. I am hoping to open in the spring of 2015, but a lot depends on timing of licensing and finalizing capital.

"The name Tidal River Brewing Company comes from the rough Algonquin translation of Connecticut which means 'On the long tidal river.'. . . Being a small nano-sized brewer is what really informs how and what I brew. I like to keep fresh and different beers on rotation, and keeping it at the 2 bbl size is going to give me a great deal of flexibility and variety I'm looking for. I'm open to suggestions and requests, too. I see this as being a deeply community-driven brewery."

Tidal River did indeed open, and it's chugging right along with the rest of the Connecticut beer machine. Geoff is wowing beer lovers with brews such as No Clever Name, described as "an English mild-style ale brewed with brown sugar for a sweet molasses backbone, fermented with English-style yeast for a nice old-world touch"; Swamp Wookie, "an American cream-ale style with a light hop aroma and bittering"; and Mayo Powered Computer, "a clean drinking blonde ale with a bready malt backbone." And you've got to love this socially conscious brewer when he posts online that the tip jar money at the tasting room goes to UNICEF. Cheers, Geoff!

Thimble Island Brewery

16 Business Park Drive
Branford, CT 06405-1890
(203) 208-2827
www.thimbleislandbrewery.com

Opened in 2012, Thimble Island has grown by leaps and bounds. From a pieced-together brewing system to moving to a larger facility and having more than a half-dozen beers available, Justin Gargano and Mike Fawcett are living the dream on Connecticut's shoreline. Their flagship

American Ale (5% ABV) is a beer that can be enjoyed year-round, as is Coffee Stout (6% ABV), a seasonal beer that became so popular, it earned a place on their year-round list. Ghost Island DIPA (7.7% ABV) also got a rave from a customer on their Facebook page.

Available throughout Connecticut at dozens of restaurants, bars, and liquor stores, there's no excuse for not trying Thimble Island's beers. I'm thinking about starting a beer run.

Thomas Hooker Brewing Company
16 Tobey Road
Bloomfield, CT 06002-3522
(860) 242-3111
www.hookerbeer.com

Lisa Bielawski is general manager of Thomas Hooker and spent some time with me discussing their history and their brews. First, the name: Thomas Hooker was a Puritan and one of the founders of Hartford, after emigrating to the colonies from England to escape persecution for nonconformity. And if there's one trait I think New Englanders possess, it's that need to march to the beat of one's own drum.

Curt Cameron is the current owner, the person responsible for growing the company to its present size and in its present location of Bloomfield, where the presence of two breweries makes for fun touring and tasting. Hooker has 16 styles of beer, some of which rotate with the seasons, and they say they "don't get trendy." For example, their autumn beer is a classic Oktoberfest in the traditional Marzen style—no pumpkin here! The beers are available in Connecticut, Massachusetts, areas of Long Island, and a small pocket of Philly.

Hooker is open Saturdays for tours and tastings as well as the first and third Fridays of the month. In the spirit of sharing the wealth, the brewery donates a portion of the Friday fees to the Village for Families and Children in Hartford, a charity Curt is closely connected with.

Two Roads Brewing Company
1700 Stratford Avenue
Stratford, CT 06615-6419
www.tworoadsbrewing.com

Phil Markowski has been brewing beer for 26 years, and his long and winding career path has led to Two Roads. As we talked one day, he told me about this two-year-old success story: "We renovated a 100-year-old manufacturing facility with an eye to having enough space at the outset so we don't have to build on or expand. Our tasting room can accommodate 200 people, plus we have an outdoor beer garden. It's open six days a week. We're literally two-tenths of a mile from I-95."

In addition to making their own beers, Two Roads is brewing beer for other companies, which helps pay for their overhead. Asked about the stigma of having someone else make your beer, Markowski says, "Even the purists are coming to ask, 'How does the beer taste?' rather than 'Where is it brewed?' We're doing our own brands before brewing anyone else's. We wanted to brew based on what we felt were underrepresented in the market. Our Workers Comp Saison, a farmhouse ale, gets us on the crest of the saison wave. Its name reflects the Belgian tradition of partly compensating the farm workers with nine liters of beer a day, since the water source was dubious. We're making it all year long in six-packs and on tap. We thought a well-made lager was lacking in the craft market. We dry-hopped our lager, which would be against the rules in Germany, but that's what we do. It's called Ol'factory Pils as a reference to our 'old factory' location. It's more pungent than a European pilsner."

Markowski commented on the upsurge in Connecticut, rather late in coming than in the rest of New England, of craft beer: "There are 33 breweries in the state and another 12 to 15 in planning. Imported beer was the king for decades, so craft beer wasn't a strong part of the culture. Now it's changing rapidly. I was here during the dark ages of craft brewing, and the mentality was, 'You make this 10 miles away. Why does it cost so much?' Now the desire for local products includes beer.

"We are a big brewery, no question. Volume-wise, we're about equal to Shipyard and Harpoon. My partners and I have collectively 40 years of beer marketing, and we knew this is the way we wanted to build this company. But we do have genuine passion for beer. Above all we want to support and promote the craft business in Connecticut and New England in general. It's a myth that you can't be big and passionate. We want to see craft breweries across the country succeed."

Amen to that.

Veracious Brewing Company

246 Main Street
Monroe, CT 06468
(203) 880-5670
www.veraciousbrewing.com

Tess and Mark Szamatulski are the authors of *Clone Brews* and *Beer Captured* and they own Maltose Express, the largest home-brew and wine-making store in the Northeast. After years of helping others brew beer, opening their own brewery made sense. Mark, an engineer-turned-home-brewer-turned-brewer, does the brewing and Tess, who had a catering business, does, in her words, everything else.

Veracious Brewing Company, whose slogan is "The Truth Is in the Beer," is open and sometimes brews twice in one day. Their tasting room is set up like an English pub, with a fireplace, cornhole, and darts in addition to church pews and a table made from a 200-year-old baptismal font, compliments of one of their customers who was taking apart a church. Watch the video on YouTube, courtesy of Booze 4 News, where Tess and Mark tell their story. And get down to the tasting room for some of their up to 12 beers, including Grady's Better Bitter (Grady is their handsome golden retriever), an English pale ale. Veracious also serves eight wines by the glass and has a bring-your-own-food policy, providing menus for local restaurants so you can order and have the food delivered.

Willimantic Brewing Company / Main Street Café
967 Main Street
Willimantic, CT 06226-2330
(860) 423-6777
www.willibrew.com

"We always planned to open a brewery," says owner David Wollner. "We looked at old mills, but wanted the building to have some character of its own. We didn't want a strip mall or a TGI Fridays with kitschy things hanging off the walls. In 1993 a local restaurant closed and we bought it, and opened it as a craft beer bar, called Main Street Café. There was a lot of good local beer like Shipyard and Harpoon and we had 20 taps. We opened the brewery in the current location in the post office in February 1997. I hired a consultant named Blair Potts, who used to brew for New Haven Brewing. He built the brewery with equipment made by New England Brewing Systems.

"I source as many ingredients as I can locally, and am partnering with a farmer who'll be growing hops for me for the next two years. It's terrific that this will drive people back into farming. If people buy local, everyone prospers."

Willibrew, as it's fondly called by regulars, boasts 40 taps, mostly New England brewed with some West Coast brands thrown in, and sells 800 barrels of its own beer per year. "Consumers are much more savvy and won't drink what they would have 20 years ago," Wollner says. "I had time to learn and a restaurant that helped support the business."

Wollner is not the first brewpub owner to admit that the state's new laws allowing beer to be sold in tasting rooms without food might be the model he'd have chosen if allowed back in 1991. " But I want to offer food," he explains. "Customers are having a couple of beers then going to get something to eat. We have such a diverse menu, we offer both a dining experience and good beers." Willibrew has a real-deal chef in Will Deason, a graduate of the Johnson & Wales culinary arts program, and a wide menu. "We are a destination because we serve food," according to Wollner. "We're easily found in the quiet corner of northeastern Connecticut, about an hour from Providence, 30 minutes from casinos."

Connecticut Beer Bus Tour

CT Beer Trail Brewery Bus Tours
(860) 292-0279
www.ctbeertrail.net

Bryon Turner was gracious to have me aboard as a special guest on one of his tours, and he gives an exhaustive tour, believe me! He also runs the CT Beer Trail website, and it's up-to-date and interactive. Get on and get informed about all things beer in the Nutmeg State.

Maine

"The way life should be" is Maine's slogan, and "Crack one open!" is that of D.L. Geary's, the first craft brewery in Maine (1986) and the first east of the Mississippi. It's heartening to know that the first state to enact a law prohibiting the making of alcohol was also the first to start making it again as soon as it could after the big "P."

The beer scene in Maine is vibrant, if not explosive. As we go to print, there are rumored to be 75 breweries and brewpubs here. I say "rumored" because you can get on any list, that of the Maine Brewers Guild or *Yankee Brew News* or Wikipedia or the Brewers Association, and get different figures. It's happening that fast, so I've done my best to get as many breweries in the book as I can. I congratulate our state's lawmakers for working with our brewers, farmers, and maltsters to change laws that enlarge this field and who recognize that beer-making is becoming a big part of many region's economies. And to the brewers, farmers, and maltsters, keep pushing for better laws that make your jobs easier in order to bring us great beer.

Although I have my own Maine beer experiences, I want to open this chapter with a piece by my friend "Hophead," who blogs about beer at Beer-Journal (www.beer-journal.com). I recommend it for information and photos of his travels throughout the three northern New England states: Maine, Vermont, and New Hampshire. Hophead's quick assessments of some of Maine's craft beers follow:

Maine Beer Company. Period. Their hoppy American Ales are a must. Dinner, a double IPA, is a masterpiece. Of the Industrial Way breweries, Bissell is my favorite. Soon, they are going to explode. Absolutely explode. Rising Tide makes American style beers. Daymark and Zephyr are their best in my opinion. Bunker Brewing is notable. They recently became more consistent with their beers, and their space is incredible. Sebago Brewing is part of the old guard in Maine, but they're working their behinds off to stay current with new beers. Banded Horn in Biddeford is about to erupt as well. Great back story, great location, great beers. People seem to like Funky Bow beers a lot. In'finiti [now named Liquid Riot] does some really cool small batch beers in their brew pub. Plus, the space is amazing. People go nuts for Oxbow's Farmhouse ales . . . a very creative company.

That's just one person's opinion, so get ready to visit and judge for yourself!

Airline Brewing Company–Amherst
22 Mill Lane
Amherst, ME 04605
(207) 584-2337
www.abcmaine.beer

Airline Brewing used to be Square Tail until 2016, when ownership changed hands. I talked with prior owner Wes Ellington, and he assured me that although he no longer is brewing as Square Tail, he's going to keep up his home-brew practice. Best of luck, Wes! As for the new owners, they have been busy traveling about England, touring breweries such as Marston's, Theakston's, and Wadsworth's. There's some serious beer knowledge being shared there! Not only that, they are busy getting a building fitted out in Ellsworth, Maine. See the following write-up for that one.

Amherst is a short drive from Bangor, so you can fit in a nice tour of local breweries in Bangor, Brewer, or Orono on a day you visit Airline. The Growler Bus (www.thegrowlerbus.com) has a trip there, too, called An Amherst Adventure, if you want to leave the driving to Gene Beck and his crew.

Airline Brewing Company–Ellsworth

173 Main Street
Ellsworth, ME 04605
(207) 584-2337
www.abcmaine.beer

Going with the flow of beer, Airline announced that its Ellsworth location would open in mid-June 2016. Ellsworth is the beautiful "gateway" to Acadia National Park and Bar Harbor, so any trip to those gorgeous Maine destinations is an excuse to swing into Airline and try their beers. Check their Facebook page for updates, grand opening news, and beer styles being made.

Allagash Brewing Company

50 Industrial Way
Portland, ME 04103-1270
(207) 878-5385
www.allagash.com

That was then: In 1996 I wrote this about the new Belgian brewery in town:

Rob Tod has never home-brewed a batch of beer in his life. He preferred to jump right into the microbrew fray, opening Allagash in 1995 and offering his Belgian-style beers to Greater Portland aficionados. His decision to brew on a bigger scale, however, was not without much preparation. Tod, who hails from Carlisle, Massachusetts, graduated from Middlebury College with a degree in geology. After a few years of traveling, he returned to Vermont, where he went to work at Otter Creek Brewing Company.

"It was supposed to be a part-time job," Tod explains, "but the company was growing so quickly, my position grew from washing kegs to learning all aspects of the micro business—from cleaning tanks, brewing, and bottling to doing lab work. I did just about everything while I was there."

Why did Tod choose Portland, Maine, as a site for his brewery? And why Belgians? The twenty-seven-year-old has his reasons: "I saw

Portland as an area for good growth potential. There is a keen awareness among local beer drinkers about microbrewed beers, a lot of interest, and more people to drink it than some other places in northern New England. And no one there was making Belgian-style beers. My choice to brew Belgians is based partly on love for the styles and partly on marketing," says Tod. "They are distinctive and unique, yet accessible and very drinkable—and, again, no one else was making them here."

This is now: Rob Tod is a bit older now, and wiser. He not only met the goals he set out to accomplish back in 1995, but exceeded them beyond all expectations. Slow and steady wins the race. In an interview I conducted with Rob one beautiful summer day, he talked about "the good old days of craft beer."

Neither one of us can fathom that it's been so long since I last drove to the Riverton section of Portland to interview Rob and take photos of the brewery. It's like visiting a museum. Allagash has grown so much bigger since he opened it. "In fact," Rob said, "just to remind ourselves of the scale of the first brewing system to the huge system we have now, we had someone paint outlines of the vessels on the concrete floor of the first brewery." I'm here to tell you it's mind-boggling to see the growth and expansion. The first humble building is in the back of the newer one, and Rob told me that their newest expansion will connect the buildings.

We sat outside that warm August day in the Allagash patio area, where some happy beer-drinkers played cornhole and others just basked in the glow of late summer sun and a cold beer. When I asked him to reminisce about "the good old days," Rob sipped his beer then said, "There were no good old days, really. We struggled for a long time to educate beer drinkers to what a Belgian was and what it was supposed to taste like. It probably took 10 years until we knew we were going to make it." I asked about whether they gave tours back then. "We offered tours, but no one came." We laugh. The tasting room today is packed with people of all ages, sipping, chatting, texting, and lining up for tours. Good things come to those who wait.

Riverton is about a $20 cab ride from downtown, so share a cab and plan on visiting Geary's, too, as well as three newer breweries (all opened in 2014) down the road apiece: Bissell Brothers, Austin Street, and Foundation. (Note that Bissell Brothers will move to Thompson's Point, Portland, in 2016.)

Andrew's Brewing Company
353 High Street
Lincolnville, ME 04849-5846
(207) 763-3305

That was then: In 1995, owner/brewer Andy Hazen happily reported that his microbrewed beers were in such demand that distributors begged him to bottle the stuff. Called "a national treasure" by Maine columnist and beer devotee Al Diamon, Andrew's beers were available on tap in Portland at Three Dollar Dewey's, the Great Lost Bear, and Bleachers. Due to the diligence of his distributors, it would soon be available throughout Maine. Hazen chuckles when he quotes Diamon's assessment of his Pale Ale: "hoppy enough to stun a rhino." With production climbing steadily at 100 percent a year, it wouldn't be long before Hazen broke down, bought a bottling line and shipped to the other New England states. After all, a "national treasure" begs to be appreciated on a regional scale.

This is now: Although Andy Hazen and his son Ben still brew beer here, Andy urges people to go to his new place, Andy's Brew Pub at the Lobster Pound (see the following listing). The original Andrew's is essentially in a garage, and on a day Ben is bottling, a surprise visit can interrupt their flow.

Andy's Brew Pub at the Lobster Pound
2521 Atlantic Highway
Lincolnville, ME 04849
Lobster Pound, (207) 789-5500; Brew Pub, (207) 763-3305
www.lobsterpoundmaine.com

Andrew's Brewing Company never gave tours and still doesn't. But the big news is that in 2014 Andy Hazen and his son Ben began their new venture, Andy's Brew Pub, contained within the Lobster Pound, a 58-year-old lobster and seafood eatery on Lincolnville Beach. On a visit a few months after they opened, I got to see the cozy brewpub with its long, curved bar. There is table seating, too, and the large windows allow a view out to Penobscot Bay. Ben is the brewmaster at the new place, giving Andy a long-deserved and stellar venue in which to showcase his delicious beers. If you're traveling the coast of Maine anytime soon, you've got lobstah here, either steamed or in sliders, along with any number of beers to pair with it.

Atlantic Brewing Company
15 Knox Road
Bar Harbor, ME 04609-7770
(207) 288-2337
www.atlanticbrewing.com

That was then: The ales served at the Lompoc Café in downtown Bar Harbor became so popular that Doug Maffucci had to open a brewery to maintain adequate supply for the customers who wanted to take these brews home. From a one-barrel system in 1990, Atlantic Brewing Company has expanded to produce 50,000 gallons of brewer Roger Normand's five styles of ale per year. Content to market their beers only in Maine, Maffucci and Normand and crew serve up their eclectic menu, both food and beers, during the height of the tourist season from May through October.

The beers: Bar Harbor Blueberry Ale, each batch made with 200 pounds of Maine wild blueberries; Ginger Wheat Ale, a summer-style ale hopped with fresh ginger, yielding a crisp ginger aroma and dry finish; Coal Porter, an assertive porter offering generous hopping and malt body, this ale is cellared to create a mocha, smoky quality in the aroma; Bar Harbor Real Ale, a smoothly sweet, nut brown ale, lightly hopped.

This is now: Atlantic was never legally connected to Lompoc Café, but Doug Maffucci did make his beer on that property. Lompoc still exists, and I urge you to dine there when you're in Bar Harbor. It's seasonal, so check the website (www.lompoccafe.com) for hours and opening dates. As for Atlantic Brewing Company, its production has grown over the years and it's now located a bit of a ways out of town on Knox Road. The facility has a beer garden in season and a roomy tasting area, with lots of merchandise to bring back to wherever home is.

In an interview I had with Doug and his lovely daughter Enrica, who helps out when she can, I found out that he bought out Bar Harbor Brewing Company several years ago from owners Todd and Suzi Foster. Bar Harbor made award-winning beers and were well-respected in the beer community. Doug still makes Bar Harbor's beers, including my favorite, Cadillac Mountain Stout, with the same recipes, making his lineup of beers varied and still amazing after all these years.

Commenting about how things have changed in the craft beer world, Doug said, "People are much less forgiving now about variations in a beer. Quality and consistency are far more important to us now than rapid growth."

Austin Street Brewery

1 Industrial Way, Suite 8
Portland, ME 04103-1072
(207) 200-1994
www.austinstreetbrewery.com

This was the third stop on our Maine Brew Bus tour, and it was the first time partners and owners Jake Austin and Will Fisher were pouring their beer publicly. This is the great "rush" for being on one of Zach Poole's tours: He often sets up special visits with brewers that the general public just doesn't get. We were a motley crew of about 30, but Jake poured like a pro and we soon all held glasses of beer to sip while they talked about their new venture.

I blogged about this experience at What's Brewing in Maine (www .whatsbrewing.bangordailynews.com) and interviewed the pair a week later.

Who the heck is Brett Anomyces?

He's not tall, dark, and handsome. He's not a long drink of water, and he's not the latest TV serial killer or even a recently optioned pitcher for the Red Sox. So then, who the heck IS Brett Anomyces? Be patient. If you know Brett, don't blurt it out in front of the others, and if you don't know who this slippery character is, read on.

I was privileged recently to be a special guest on the lime green Maine Brew Bus named "Lenny," as we visited four new Maine breweries: Banded Horn in Biddeford and three in the same industrial park in Portland. Among them was Austin Street Brewery, a fledgling one-barrel system awaiting its final approval by the State of Maine before rolling out their first brews.

In an interview I was able to get later, the guys talked via speaker phone, and Jake explained, "Brettanomyces is a type of wild yeast used to make a saison, which is traditionally a Belgian style. Americans have embraced the style in the past few years. The aroma depends on how you're using the Brett. If you are using it in primary fermentation, it's milder, but if you're using it in the secondary fermentation, you might get horse blanket, wet hay, funkiness."

Ahh. Mystery man revealed. "Brett" used to be anathema in a brewery. Now brewers are deliberately going for that unique funk.

Jake says, "It's not for everyone, but the first time I tasted a beer like that, I fell in love." He thinks that first beer that influenced his attempt here was probably Allagash Confluence.

Austin Street is waiting on one last approval from the State before they roll out the two flagship beers, Patina Pale Ale and Lawnmower. Using a tiny, 1 bbl system that produces 31-gallon batches, the pair guarantee they will go to a bigger system at some point. "It takes the same time to brew a small batch of beer as a larger one," Jake says, laughing.

How did they meet? Will is Jake's brother-in-law. Jake had been home-brewing for five years, and both he and Will wanted to take on an entrepreneurial project. Will said, "Jake has the skills, I wanted to own a business, and we play off each other's skill sets to make it all come together."

Note: Austin Street celebrated two years in business in April 2016 and has expanded production with a new 10 bbl system. The more beer, the better!

The Bag and Kettle
Sugarloaf Mountain
19 Village West
Carrabassett Valley, ME 04947
(207) 237-2451
www.thebagandkettle.com

Opened in 1969, "The Bag" has long served great pub food and in-house-brewed beers to skiers at Sugarloaf. Beers include Trout Brook Pale Ale, a low-carb beer (sign me up!); Uncle's Winter, with a rich, dark malt body and a "bright" finish; Joe Stout, made with espresso beans; and The Bag's Potato Ale, described as "a full-bodied, lightly hopped ale that achieves its well-balanced flavor from locally grown Yukon gold potatoes." The menu has everything you would expect at a great pub: rib-sticking burgers and sandwiches as well as salads, soups, and gluten-free options. "Baggers can be choosers," the menu states.

Banded Horn Brewing Co.
32 Main Street, Building 13-W
Biddeford, ME 04005-5173
(207) 602-1561
www.bandedhorn.com

There's nothing like getting to share in the pride of watching nice guys pour their first beers for a thirsty crowd of beer bus tour-goers. Who cares that it's 11 in the morning? It's 5 o'clock somewhere. Ian McConnell and partner Ron Graves welcomed us into their gigantic space in the Pepperell Mill in downtown Biddeford on a wet, bone-chillingly cold day in February 2014.

There was a lot of clicking of cameras as some media rode along to get their scoops and a few samples. I managed to get off a few shots myself—photos, that is. The guys talked about their backgrounds and what inspired the beers Ian was brewing. When asked about the name of the brewery, Ian held up a large curved horn, like the kind you blow when trying to send a signal in some remote land. "We just thought it was a cool name," he said, sheepishly.

Working with a 22-barrel system, Ian has been busy since that cold winter's day, brewing over a half-dozen beers that range from a 4.6% ABV Keller pils called Pepperell Pilsener to a 12% ABV Russian imperial stout called Mountain. In between are some really interesting styles.

Baxter Brewing Co.
70 Lincoln Street
Lewiston, ME 04240
(207) 333-6769
www.baxterbrewing.com

On the day I spoke with him, Luke Livingston, owner of Baxter Brewing, was headed home from Connecticut, stuck in traffic on I-495. I've found that this is the best time to catch brewers and owners: when they can't run away from me. Being nosy, I asked Luke what he was doing in the Nutmeg State, to which he replied, "I was meeting with potential distributors in Rhode Island, Connecticut, New York City, New Jersey, Maryland, and Washington, DC, and what I don't know at this point [August 2014] is which of those collaborations will come to fruition. We're currently available in four New England states: Maine, Vermont, New Hampshire, and Massachusetts."

The first brewery in New England to can all of its beer, Baxter underwent a 400 percent expansion of its brewery in 2013. "We expanded capacity outside, adjacent to our existing space, added a second canning line, and renovated the second floor for offices," Luke said. "We've also rented an 8,500-square-foot warehouse that contains a 2,500-square-foot cooler. Distributors now pick up the beer there. The tasting room has also been enlarged, so there's more room to enjoy the beer."

What sets apart the Baxter Brewing tasting room experience? Luke says without hesitating, "We're located in a historic, 170-year-old textile mill that in its time was the largest employer in Maine. That mill produced tents and uniforms for the Grand Army of the Potomac in the Civil War."

Having visited Baxter at Bates Mill #6, albeit before the expansion, I can vouch for its unique location and tasting room experience. The staff is friendly and accommodating and make it a fun tour. This mill building was once a falling-down wreck, but the renovation that added the brewery, as well as offices, restaurants, and other tenants, has made this corner of Lewiston glow again. Right downstairs is locally owned Fish Bones American Grill (www.fishbonesag.com), open for lunch and dinner. Taste the beer upstairs and enjoy an eclectic menu and more beer right in the same building.

Belfast Bay Brewing Company

100 Searsport Avenue
Belfast, ME 04915-7221
(207) 338-4216
www.belfastbaybrewing.com

When I first spoke with owner Pat Mullen, he had just hired Dan McGovern, former owner of Lake St. George Brewing Company, to be his brewer. Well, Dan and his son-in-law have since moved to Monhegan Island, where they've opened their own brewery, and because Belfast Bay's beers were in such high demand, Pat decided to turn over production to Shipyard Brewing Company. "I was selling 80 to 90 cases on my own, which meant staying up half the night to get the cases packed up," he says. "Shipyard can make 940 cases in two hours, so with this program I could make all the beer I could sell. We're now available in 13 states and five different countries. People call us from all over asking where they can buy our beers."

"Belfast Bay Lobster Ale and McGovern's Oatmeal Stout are the only two beers we make, and people are happy with that." Mullen chuckles, "The only thing is, I have to explain to a lot of people that 'no lobsters have been harmed in the making of this beer.'" With brewers putting oysters in stout now, no wonder folks are asking.

One of the challenges Mullen faces is that he doesn't have a place where people can come to taste the beers. Recovering from a recent stroke, he has decided to turn over the company to his daughter Marci. "I've got to slow down," he said, "but she's looking to the future, and has some new ideas." Stay tuned, because I think there may be a tasting room in their future. Check out their website to find their offerings in bars and restaurants and support great beer, even if you can't visit the tasting room.

Bigelow Brewing Company

473 Bigelow Hill Road
Skowhegan, ME 04976-5126
(207) 399-6262
www.bigelowbrewing.com

I first visited Bigelow on the day of their grand opening in May 2014, and it was, well, grand. Housed in a renovated horse barn a few dozen yards from their home, Pam and Jeff Powers had made this a family effort. At the time, both had day jobs, as do many small brewers, so the results of their efforts were even more rewarding. Hundreds of people came by to congratulate the couple, listen to live music, and chow down on the nice spread. Pam made donut holes with the Lying Bastard Pale Ale . . . little orbs of yum. The converted barn was drop-dead gorgeous—Jeff and some friends did it themselves, and I've rarely seen such beautiful, precise woodwork—and there was a tasting area for growler fills and samples.

When I visited again, I got a delightful surprise: Pam and Jeff have already built a 50-foot extension onto the barn to expand the brewing capacity. They have also built a to-die-for outdoor pizza oven that turned out a delicious pie with chicken, pesto, and marinated feta. They have live music some nights; check their Facebook page for details. Pam has now left teaching and is working full-time in the Bigelow brewing and food business. There's more to come, but I have to keep it under my hat for now.

Since opening in 2014, Bigelow has expanded its brewing capacity fourfold and is distributing its beer. The Powers are a great example of hard-working craft brewers who just can't make enough beer for the demand. That's a great problem to have.

Here's the recipe for those donut holes (I have no idea why they are called Okinawan Donuts, but you can ask Pam or Jeff when you see them!):

Okinawan Donuts
Mix together:
3 cups flour
1 cup granulated sugar
3 teaspoons baking powder
1 teaspoon salt
1 teaspoon vanilla
2 eggs
¾ cup milk
¾ cup Lying Bastard Pale Ale
1 teaspoon nutmeg

Heat vegetable oil to 375 degrees F.
Drop balls of dough 1" in diameter into hot oil, being careful not to get splattered; donuts will float to the top. Fry until done all the way through. Might have to sample to check.
Roll in granulated sugar. Enjoy!
Yield: about 3 dozen

Bissell Brothers Brewing
4 Thompson's Point Road, Suite 108
Portland, ME 04102
(207) 808-8258
www.bissellbrothers.com

All aboard the Maine Brew Bus, on that legendary day when Peter and Noah Bissell, and their mom and dad, greeted "the swarm," as I like to think of our crowd off the bus. Open for only two months at that time, the guys were pumped to have such an eager crowd, and they put on quite a show. Peter joked about Noah's first home-brewing attempt: "It tasted like something that came out of the bottom of an ashtray." But like all of us who have had home-brew disasters, Noah has gotten things fine-tuned in that department. The reaction to Bissell Brothers beer has been explosive. There are usually lines out the door for growler fills.

Beers include The Substance (6.6% ABV), their flagship, described as "a brightly dank ale that threads many needles"; Baby Genius (4% ABV), "a hoppy, hazy session beer"; and the robust Bucolia Amber Ale (5.6% ABV), described as "sticky hops layered over soft malt." In 2016 the guys will move to a much larger space at Thompson's Point in Portland, a tribute to their "baby genius" and great brews.

Black Bear Brewery
19 Mill Street, Suite 4
Orono, ME 04473-4095
(207) 949-2880
www.blackbearmicrobrew.com

"It's all about the beer here," brewer Tim Gallon says, when I asked him if he serves food. "We have popcorn and sell pizza by the slice from the Bear, and the Family Dog brings over burgers and hot dogs." Obviously, people don't mind that Gallon's taproom, which opened in 2012, isn't also a restaurant. "We get lots of support from professors, students, and locals," he says. "Everyone from all walks of life loves local beer."

To give a bit of the history, Tim started out at the Bear Brewpub, owned then by Milos Blagojevic. The Bear no longer brews beer—Tim is happy to supply them with what they need of his—but they are still there, serving great pub food (as Andy Hazen told me in the first *What's Brewing*). However, there's no official affiliation. The Maine black bear is the mascot of the University of Maine sports teams, hence the moniker used by both college-town places.

Tim incorporated in 2004 while brewing at the Bear, then opened in 2007. "I learned from Milosz," he said, "and learned on my own as well. We built it from the ground up. The building used to be a supermarket. After it closed, we got a lease and built out BBB." Some of the beers Tim makes are: Tough End IPA, a nod to their location, which was long ago considered the tough end of town; Big Di'pah, a double IPA; and a red IPA called The Ri'pah. Gallon (should he change his name to "Growler"??) likes the new model of being able to ease off the process of getting a beer into a distributor's hands and brewing and serving it in the taproom. They still distribute on tap throughout Maine, but this allows Tim to spend time with the people drinking his beer.

Boothbay Craft Brewery
301 Adams Pond Road
Boothbay, ME 04537-4334
(207) 633-3411
www.boothbaycraftbrewery.com

Located on the grounds of the long-running Boothbay Resort, Boothbay Craft Brewery boasts its atmosphere as its most valuable asset. The Watershed Tavern is open seasonally for now, but the brewery produces beer year-round. And since opening, they've increased production 400 percent and are self-distributing in some areas of the state. Here's a new one on me: They can some of their beer in 32-ounce cans called "crowlers."

Long and sorely needed in Boothbay was a tavern with house-brewed beer—a place to gather, toast the newly arrived spring, toast getting through winter, or toast just gathering itself. The menu may look like pub fare, but quality shrieks its name from the print: wood-fired pizzas, burgers, panini, appetizers like house-made charcuterie plates, award-winning seafood chowder, and entrees such as cedar-planked salmon, baked stuffed haddock, and chicken potpie in a skillet.

As for the beer, try Win Mitchell's four regulars and others, some collaboration brews, that rotate. I'm looking at a barrel-aged New England imperial stout served in a snifter. That will be for when I'm not driving home. Their flagship is the 633 Pale Ale (6.33% ABV), described as "a mildly hoppy pale ale using 2-row, Vienna, caramel, and Munich malts for body, color, and head retention. It is hopped with American west coast hops later in the boil giving it a nice citrus hop flavor and very mild aroma. Slight addition of a roasted caramel malt gives 633 its signature 'sunset over the harbor glow.'" This one named itself when the ABV turned out to be the Boothbay region's telephone exchange.

Bray's Brewing Company

678 Roosevelt Trail
Naples, ME 04055-5335
(207) 693-6806
www.braysbrewpub.com

That was then: The story of how Bray's Brewpub came into being should be accompanied by the theme to *The Twilight Zone*. The way Michele Windsor tells it, she and her husband, Michael Bray, went to college in Maine, spent the next thirteen years in the Pacific Northwest, then decided to open a brewpub back in Maine. Their choice of Naples was based on such marketing principles as traffic count, visibility, area demographics, and parking availability. The 150-year-old mansard-roofed Victorian at the intersection of Routes 302 and 35 fulfilled all those requirements.

What Michele and Michael didn't know until they opened the Eatery in August 1995, was that two of the town's founding fathers shared their last names. Washington Bray and William Winsor helped settle the town of Naples more than a hundred years before, and both men had lived within a quarter-mile of the present location of the pub. (Michele points out that her name was spelled without the "d" until her great-grandfather added it eighty years ago.) Bray has been brewing at capacity since introducing his own beers in December 1995. "There are no fresher ales in the Lakes Region than this," he says. "There are no bottles, no kegs; it goes fresh from the brewery to your glass."

This is now: Michael and Michele are no longer married, and Michael owns and runs the pub now with partner Sonja. The beers include Brandy Pond Blonde, Mt. Olympus Dark IPA, Pleasant Mountain Porter, and Muddy River Bog Brown, along with a host of others that are seasonal and one-offs. Bray's also has 11 additional taps devoted to local beer for the most part.

As for the food, they still make the mussels steamed in Bray's ale with Andouille sausage and roasted pepper I tried on a long-ago New Year's Eve. This is a nice twist to the usual New England–style mussels, and if you like that Southern twist, you'll love this dish. Other appetizers, soups, and salads are pretty standard pub fare, and the entrees include house-smoked barbecued beef brisket and pulled pork, baby back ribs cooked in Bray's ale, and penne and cheese—all stick-to-the-ribs food, a perfect match with the beers.

Bunker Brewing Co.
17 Westfield Street
Portland, ME 04101
(207) 450-5014
www.bunkerbrewingco.com

Founded by Chresten Sorensen and Jay Villani in 2011, Bunker Brewing has earned huge kudos from the beer-drinking community both here and away. Take for, example, the rave they received from *Food & Wine* magazine as makers of one of the top 50 lagers in the country. *F&W* loved Machine Czech Pils, which Bunker describes as "Old-World charm in a glass. Bunker-style. Biscuity German malt meets boatloads of skunky Saaz hops."

Chresten and Jay are at the heart of the Portland brewing scene, and their brewery is a must-visit. Their move to the Westfield Street location will allow them to have a 1,000-square-foot tasting room and to expand production 200 percent. This peninsula will soon be swimming in beer!

Deep Water Brewing at the Vinery
33 Tenney Hill
Blue Hill, ME 04614-5948
(207) 374-2411
www.arborvine.com

I have fallen in love with the Blue Hill area. There isn't a brewery in Brooklin yet, but boy, did I think about opening a nanobrewery there. Get a nice one-barrel system, and I'd have my own home business. There *is* a brewpub nearby in Blue Hill called Deep Water Brewing, and that is the brainchild of Tim Hikade and his parents, who own the long-running restaurant Arborvine.

Deep Water has a tasting room, located in a 200-year-old barn moved from another location and rescued with a complete renovation. The pub is down the driveway a bit in the same house-turned-restaurant as Arborvine, a more fine-dining experience. Tim gave us a tour, then we took home a growler of Otto Lager, named for Tim's Austrian great-grandfather. This is a dark-hued lager with a nice malty resonance on the tongue—perfect with cheese and crackers on the deck.

Tim weighed in on his favorite food/beer pairing: "That would have to be the shepherd's pie and porter we were serving recently. It's not your typical shepherd's pie; with tomato, Parmesan, and an array of vegetables, this was a great fall pairing."

No matter what the season, I urge you to travel to the Blue Hill peninsula, my new favorite part of Maine, where you can sample beer at Deep Water, then drive a mile to see Al and Mia Strong at Strong Brewing in Sedgwick. It's a great place to explore, with vistas of the ocean at many turns along the road around the peninsula.

D.L. Geary Brewing Company
38 Evergreen Drive
Portland, ME 04103-1066
(207) 878-2337
www.gearybrewing.com

That was then: If one person is responsible for igniting the microbrewery fire under the East Coast, it's David Geary. In 1986, he was the first to open a non-contract micro east of the Mississippi, making him the "granddaddy" of New England microbrewing. Enjoy the D.L. Geary tour, buy some brewmania, and talk brewing with Geary and his crew, which includes daughter Kelly Geary Lucas. After that, head out to the Great Lost Bear (right down Forest Avenue) to enjoy sampling all three of the industrial park's brews: Allagash, Casco Bay, and D.L. Geary's.

This is now: Geary's is still in the industrial park way out in the Riverton section of Portland, but some things have changed. First of all, Casco Bay

Brewing no longer exists, and three darlings of craft beer have moved into the neighborhood: Foundation, Austin Street, and Bissell Brothers (which will be moving to Thompson's Point in 2016). Allagash remains. That's five breweries, all with tasting rooms, to visit in one fell swoop.

Another big event was the opening of a tasting room at Geary's, which was a long time coming and a much-welcomed addition to the tasting/taproom trend. Kelly Geary Lucas is pretty much running the company, while Dave visits accounts and otherwise shows up daily to keep an eye on things. He's still very much a fixture in the Portland and Maine beer scene and fun to talk to.

Geary's has introduced a gluten-free beer called Ixnay (Amscray Utenglay), which was the first Maine-made beer crafted to remove gluten. Of course, Geary's continues to make the well-loved favorites: Hampshire Ale, Pale Ale ("Crack one open!"), and London Porter.

Ebenezer's Brew Pub / Lively Brewing Company

112 Pleasant Street
Brunswick, ME 04011
(207) 373-1840
www.ebenezerspub.net

Home to Lively Brewing Company, Ebenezer's is a sibling pub to its predecessor in Lovell, which has been called one of the best beer bars in the world. On September 5, 2014, Chris Lively was enthroned as an Honorary Knight in the Belgian Brewers Guild for his contribution to the Belgian beer movement. He and his wife Jen transformed an existing brewpub into this "lively" enterprise.

Ben Rossignol is now doing the brewing, but when I visited Ebenezer's, I discovered an old beer acquaintance was then head brewer. Just when I thought he'd disappeared, up popped brewing master Michael LaCharite, who once owned Casco Bay Brewing and was involved with the beginnings of Baxter Brewing in Lewiston. I talked to Mike—who also created MALT (Maine Ale and Lager Tasters), a home-brew club that predated most—about his role at Ebenezer's: "We always have seven of our own beers on tap, sometimes two or three more, and have two guest taps, usually a sour and a dark beer plus several wines on tap.

To date we have brewed 27 300-gallon batches. Twenty-one of those have been different beers. We mostly focus on Belgian-style beers but also rotate in English, German, and American styles."

When I asked him to choose a favorite food and beer pairing, he said, "It's hard to say about pairing because the beers rotate so quickly. Right now it would be Dunkelstiltskin, our Munich dunkel, and a burger." Mike has moved on to his own consulting practice, setting up brewing systems for other brewers.

Check Ebenezer's Facebook page for their numerous events, including beer dinners. You are guaranteed great beer with Sir Chris and his crew.

Fore River Brewing Company
45 Huntress Avenue
South Portland, ME 04101
(207) 370-0629
www.foreriverbrewing.com

Alex Anastasoff, T. J. Hansen, and John LeGassey opened their gorgeous new brewery in the fall of 2015 in the swinging town of "SoPo." There's a tasting room that looks clean and as spare and functional as a Shaker dining hall. Long wooden tables and benches invite drinkers to imbibe community-style, and a huge woodstove keeps things warm in colder weather. Beers include one that's getting noticed by people who have visited recently: John Henry, described as "a traditional oatmeal milk stout. Brewed with English malts and hops, this beer presents with coffee and chocolate notes but with a light, drinkable body."

Foundation Brewing
1 Industrial Way, Suite 5
Portland, ME 04103-1072
(207) 370-8187
www.foundationbrew.com

On the anniversary of the birth of our nation, my husband and I got up way too early to travel to Thomaston, Maine, to watch the Fourth of July parade and have lunch with an artist cousin who bought a summer home right on the main street.

But Miss Crabby Appleton was made happier because her nice husband had bought her a large coffee before getting on the road. And the almost 90-minute trip from Waterville was made much more enjoyable because I had an appointment for an early-morning phone call to one of Maine's newer brewers, John Bonney, cofounder and owner, with Joel Mahaffey, of Foundation Brewing Company in Portland. We had met John and Joel, when we took part in a Maine Brew Bus tour of several new breweries in southern Maine. In addition to Banded Horn in Biddeford, we trekked around a small industrial park way out in the Riverton section of Portland to celebrate the launching of Foundation, as well as Bissell Brothers and Austin Street.

Catching up with John on July Fourth, I found him at the brewery, hard at work. I asked him how business was going since their opening. I was amazed by how young his voice sounds. And I'm amazed by how fast time flies these years, and how young everyone sounds except me. I'm happy the millennials are running things now, or at least will be soon.

"The biggest change," John said, "is that something that was only a goal a short time ago is now a reality. You make plans, and when you really get into it, there's a big difference."

"How so?" I asked.

"We knew this intellectually," he replied, "but we really learned that when you are brewing, or doing some other task around the brewery, that you can't leave until it's done. So if it's eight or nine at night, and you're still in the middle of some process, you know you are staying late."

Thinking there might be some really new gadget these young guys are using to keep them on task, I asked, "Is there a software that helps you stay organized?"

"We mostly use Google calendar," he said. "It helps us coordinate our schedules. It's only Joel and me here in the brewery, so we have to work hard to know what the other is doing or scheduled to do to keep things flowing smoothly. We can share the calendar and see who has what going on. That helps." And it helps me to know that I don't have to find something newer than Google calendar.

As for the beers, John said, "We are staying with our two beers, Eddy and Blaze, for a while, although we do have a summer saison called Wanderlust. Eddy and Blaze are examples of what we are about as a brewery. The 5% ABV makes Blaze easy to drink, and you can have a couple with dinner because they are low in alcohol. We'll definitely expand the list in the future." (Note, the brewery does offer seasonal and small-batch brews at different times.)

Joel and John met at Central Street Market in Bangor and began home brewing together. "We make a good team," John said, "because Joel is more intuitive and my background is in biochemistry, so it's a great combination for recipe development." Trained as a medical doctor, and once practicing in Waterville, John's career shift is a serious one. He told me, "I'm no longer practicing as a family physician. We've moved down here and I'm consulting so I can dedicate myself to the company."

"Are you going to be able to get away today and enjoy the holiday?" I asked. I could hear a slight chuckle. "No. I'm here for the day. Got a lot to do."

We say good-bye, and I smile and sip the coffee that will wake me up by the time we arrive at the parade route. I said to my husband, "What a nice young guy. That's what the spirit of the Fourth of July means to me. Hard work, dedication, and working to be self-sufficient." Among many other things.

Friars' Brewhouse & Bakehouse
21 Central Street (Bakehouse)
Bangor, ME 04401-5105
(207) 947-3770

Let's clear up one thing right away: The address listed above is for the Bakehouse, a little cafe in downtown Bangor. The Brewhouse is located at the Saint Elizabeth Monastery on Orcutt Mountain in Bucksport. Tours of the Brewhouse are not available except as part of a special event. Watch the Friars' Brewhouse Facebook page for those.

Who's brewing up this heavenly beer? Brother Donald Paul of the Franciscan Brothers of St. Elizabeth of Hungary, a trained chef, and his colleagues Brothers Kenneth and Stephan. And they are causing quite a stir. There is the Whoopie Pie Porter, named after Brother Donald's popular chocolate and cream cakes sold at the Bakehouse. Then there's the Saint Francis, an English-style brown ale. Both went on sale in the fall of 2014 at the Bangor Wine & Cheese Company in Bangor.

Brother Donald told Emily Burnham of the *Bangor Daily News*, "I've been brewing beer for about five years, but of course I've been working with grain and yeast and water for a very, very long time . . . You put those three things together in different ways and you get either beer or bread. It was really a pretty natural progression." As for monks brewing beer, "It's a great monastic custom. There's centuries of brewing behind us," said Brother Don. "And if you drink two liters of nine percent beer, you will have conversations with the saints as well. They'll show right up in your living room and sit down and chat with you." Oh, and at Christmas, the Brothers made a St. Nicholas Ale!

Funky Bow Brewery & Beer Company
21 Ledgewood Lane
Lyman, ME 04002-7376
(888) 456-2345
www.funkybowbeercompany.com

Where the heck is Lyman? Glad you asked. A tiny town of about 4,400 people, Lyman is in southern Maine, not exactly on the beaten path. That's why, I hazard a guess, brewmaster Paul Lorrain offers pizza: a reward for making the way to his brewery. Actually, Paul brews with his son Abraham, and once the brewery was up and running (with beers that get raves), they began Funky Bow Bread and Pizza Company. Growler nights up on the hill involve beer, live music, and wood-fired pizza. The dough is handmade with spent grain from the brewery. For an out-of-the-way brewery, people flock here when it's open. Make the pilgrimage.

The beer? Here's their description of the So Folkin' Hoppy IPA (6.5% ABV), available year-round: "A delicious hoppy IPA. A generous addition of hops with a kiss of malt sweetness balances this IPA very well. The nose is upfront with the galaxy hops, lending nuances of grapefruit, pine, and tropical notes." I absolutely love the G-String Pale Ale, and even had Central Street Farmhouse put together a "clone" kit so I can brew it at home.

Geaghan Brothers Brewing Company
34 Abbott Street
Brewer, ME 04412
(207) 945-3730
www.geaghans.com

Geaghan Brothers' brewery expanded to a new facility in, fittingly, Brewer in May 2015 and has up to 15 tap lines running when the tasting room is open, plus live music some nights. I got Andy Geaghan on the phone, right before the expansion took place. He said, "The building is a portion of the J.K. Nissen building that was used as a bakery for many years. We've done all the plumbing and electric and will be putting in a 20 bbl system and 40 bbl fermentors. Our two places combined will have the capacity to produce 4,200 barrels. We'll keep the 5 bbl brewhouse at the pub for one-offs and specialties. The Brewer facility beers will be distributed throughout the northern part of the state. We're going to stick with our regular lineup: Refueler, Smiling Irish Bastard, Presque Isle Blonde, and some IPAs from time to time. In the last three years we've made over 31 different beers out of the brewpub. The mass production will be of those mainstay beers that have proven to be winners."

I asked Andy about the policeman pictured on the label of Smiling Irish Bastard: "Bernie Welch is an old Bangor police officer who married my grandfather's sister. He's an old Bangor story, so we thought it fitting to name this beer after him. We try to tell stories of Bangor. This is where we're from, and our beers pay homage to the city's character, which is creative and no-nonsense and in a lot of ways still a blue-collar town. We're part of a rebirth of Bangor, and it's a nice to be part of.

"We're just doing our thing. We love the community of the beer culture and to meet people who are crafting great beers and enjoying them. We're passionate about the beer we're creating, but equally passionate about the relationships that come out of it."

Geaghan's Pub

570 Main Street
Bangor, ME 04401-6821
(207) 945-3730
www.geaghans.com

The day I stopped at Geaghan's Pub, the iconic tavern and restaurant that's anchored Bangor since 1975, I got a chance to survey the landscape of a happy crowd enjoying the bar and dining room, even in midafternoon. Any time seems to be the best time to have a meal or a beer at this multigenerational, family-owned eatery.

Andy Geaghan emerged from the brewery, which opened in 2011, shook my hand, and within 60 seconds of my telling him about this book, asked me if I'd like to appear on a radio show the following morning to talk about it on the air. That's the type of guy Andy is: sweet, welcoming, and with a beard that rivals that of Santa Claus, jolly. Yes, I said "jolly."

Check out their menu online and follow them on Facebook, where you'll periodically catch a glimpse into the kitchen, where their bread is baked fresh and the prime rib rubbed before it goes into the oven.

Gneiss Brewing

94 Patterson Road
Limerick, ME 04048-4242
(207) 793-004
www.gneissbeer.com

From my blog post published on July 27, 2014:

Today is a Hallmark card type of summer day in Maine, one of those days you wish you could string out to last at least a month: blue skies, clouds you could lie in a hammock and gaze at for hours and a spot-on eighty degrees with no humidity. While vacationers and tourists amble along the beach, or hike a high trail, one hardworking brewer was not taking it easy.

Tim Bissell, director of marketing and outreach at Gneiss (pronounced nice) brewery in Limerick, was manning the tasting room waiting for anyone who might arrive to refill a growler with one of Gneiss' wheat beers. Tim and owner/brewer Dustin Johnson began brewing Gneiss beer less than a year ago, and have already gotten some good traction getting it into Maine bars and restaurants.

I asked Tim how the beers have been received. "The first six months was really about educating people about our style of beers and the flavors associated with them. They're made with wheat, and a lot of people have pre-conceived notions of whether they like wheat beer or not. We just tell them, 'Just give our beers a try and see what you think.' We've had more positive than negative reviews."

He went on to explain why they chose to brew this particular style. "We really liked the German style of brewing, the balance. Some American beers can be high alcohol and highly hopped. We wanted to come at it from a different approach, which created a niche. We tell bars that this is a local beer and it's distinct and will stand out on your taps."

The farm where the brewery is located is a working farm. In addition to brewing beer, the two grow their own food using sustainable farming practices. They even have pigs that help move the dirt around. "The brewery was built on a spot that was all forest three years ago. We had it logged and built the brewery. Instead of rototilling, we raise four to five pigs a year and they root around, eat what they can find, rip up roots, turn the land over, makes piles of rocks for us. We'll clear it out next year and grow on it."

They are also growing their own hops, including Cascade, Centennial, Nugget and Magnum, with the help of Doles Orchard nearby. "Dustin has been here four years, getting a head start. We had some growing in pots in Orono, and right now have 26 hop plants, enough to harvest for two seven-barrel batches of beer."

I asked if they'd chosen a name for the harvest beers they planned on brewing in September. I can "hear" Tim smiling on the other end of the line. "No, we haven't chosen names yet. Sometimes the name comes before the beer, and sometimes it comes after the beer is made. We've even decided on a name for a new beer on the way to deliver it. It's just how creativity works."

Both Tim and Dustin are University of Maine at Orono grads but have known each other since junior high. They homebrewed after they moved off-campus. "Dustin has a strong science background, so he can take my crazy ideas and know how to make them work. He's got a great knack for combining and balancing initial and residual flavors and puts his focus on good drinkability."

What food goes well with, say, the Gneiss Weiss flagship beer? "Anything German, but seafood goes well, too. The flavors don't compete with the food, like a highly hopped beer would. It's crisp and refreshing."

I think a trip to Limerick is on my list. Although you can get the beer in local bars (see their website for particulars), if you make the trip, you can take home a growler full. They have five taps in the tasting room, which is part of the brewery. Tim quips, "I just tell people when they come, if they want to tour the brewery, just turn around in a circle, and you've seen it. It's 500 square feet, but we use every inch of it."

Tim adds, "We're certified Mainers." So support your local brewery!

Gritty McDuff's–Auburn

68 Main Street
Auburn, ME 04210-5812
(207) 376-2739
www.grittys.com

This location of the iconic Gritty's is right in downtown Auburn and is set up with warm, dark wood tables and windows that look out back to the river. It's also the official brewpub of the Dempsey Challenge. Every year the brewer cooks up a special beer to celebrate and raise money for the Dempsey Center for Hope and Healing, a cancer care center set up by actor Patrick Dempsey, himself a native Mainer, in honor of his mother, who passed away after a decades-long battle with cancer. But each year fund-raising for others goes on and includes a bike, run/walk event that furthers the center's mission to, in their words, "provide high-quality education, support and wellness services to patients, survivors and caregivers."

Gritty McDuff's–Freeport

187 Lower Main Street
Freeport, ME 04032
(207) 865-4321
www.grittys.com

That was then: The Freeport Gritty's has been packing them in since its opening in July 1995. Located about a half mile from L.L. Bean's, Gritty's features a slightly different menu than the Portlaud location, emphasizing traditional pub fare, grazing food, stone-oven pizzas, chili, burgers, sandwiches, and salads. I can attest to the satisfaction level of the club sandwiches. My eleven-year-old son Burke wanted two sandwiches. "One isn't going to fill me up, Mum," he argued. After laboring over a single, enormous turkey and bacon club, which was served with thick, wavy potato chips, he almost had to be carried out to the car. If one sandwich can fill that kid's stomach, it's a bargain at any price.

This is now: Gritty's is still there, right down the road from more outlet shops than you could get to in a week, let alone a day. Enjoy the bar, where you can peek into the glassed-in brewery below, or the spacious dining room, both lined with long pub tables, just like in the UK. And that 11-year-old son? He just turned 30 in November. He once complained of the smell of my fermenting home brew, and now he helps me drink and chat about craft beers. And he can still make quick work of a club sandwich. I think that one will still be plenty, if it's from Gritty's.

Gritty McDuff's–Portland

396 Fore Street
Portland, ME 04101-4026
(207) 772-2739
www.grittys.com

The first brewpub to open east of the Mississippi River—this is the flagship!

That was then: The crash of 1987 pretty much put Gritty McDuff's owner Richard Pfeffer out of a job as a stockbroker. What else to do but open a brewpub in the heart of Portland's charming Old Port? Co-owner and brewmaster Ed Stebbins was also ready for a career change. Selling books had its appeal, but after some time living in England, Stebbins was ready to offer his own beer instead.

"Maine's Original Brewpub" is Gritty's slogan, since it was the first such brewery/pub in Maine and the first US brewpub set up by Shipyard's Alan Pugsley. In their radio commercials, Richard and Ed bill themselves as "just a couple of guys really into beer," and Gritty's is a friendly place, where "the guys" are almost always on hand and willing to have a beer with you. The oversized windows that grace this 1870 brick building overlook the harbor, and large pub tables line the dining room, inviting customers to mingle and talk over traditional pub fare.

The beer: Ed Stebbins brews McDuff's Best Bitter, Portland Head Light Pale Ale, Black Fly Stout, Lion's Pride Brown Ale, and Sebago Light Ale. Among their many honors, Richard and Ed were asked to brew a special beer to celebrate the inauguration of Maine's governor, Angus King. Teaming up with David Geary, the trio came up with "Inaugurale, Fit for A. King." The name was nothing short of brilliant, and the beer was brilliantly received at the ball, to which everyone in the state of Maine was invited.

This is now: If you think you know Gritty McDuff's in the Old Port, give this a thought: There is the rockin' Gritty's of Saturday night, when you stand shoulder to shoulder with other beer lovers, barely able to hear your friends talking, never mind the commentary on whatever game is on the TV over the bar. The noise of the crowd washes over you, and bits of laughter and anguish increase suddenly when someone's team loses. This is a communal experience, and the sound of many voices together is a language all its own.

Then there is the serene, sun-kissed Gritty's of a Monday afternoon in late March, where a few parties of two sit by the large windows and talk quietly, sipping a beer or a cup of tea, and the lone drinker at the bar contemplates whatever thought rolls around in his head at the moment.

This is the Gritty's I found on a cold, gray Monday in March 2014 when I visited for an interview with the owners, Richard Pfeffer and Ed Stebbins. I came to talk to the guys about their lives since my last book came out, the changes in the beer business in those intervening years, and their thoughts about life in general.

Although I had a page of typed-up questions to ask, our talk meandered and the conversation became an organic one, as if three friends were gathered at the local pub to catch up after a long time. That quality of a public place, a place that isn't home and isn't work, where no one expects anything of you except to relax and enjoy yourself, is what sociologist Ray Oldenburg calls "the third place." And Gritty McDuff's has it in spades.

"You're not getting all J. K. Rowling on me, are you?" Ed teases when I mention this "third place." No, there are no dragons or wizards involved. It's a quality of public gathering that people have been engaged in for hundreds of years in the bistros and cafes of Paris, the coffeehouses along the Ringstrasse in Vienna, the *enoteche* (wine bars) of Italy, and the taverns and pubs of Ireland and England.

If a place doesn't invite me to come in, spread out a book or a journal, and enjoy whatever beverage I order, whether I be in a coffeehouse like Bard in Portland, or in a pub like Gritty's, it's a place I don't return to.

There is a slight buzz of voices, the music is just the right volume, and the temperature is cozy and warm in winter (preferably with a fireplace or gas stove) and not so air-conditioned in summer that you're driven to wish you had a shawl to wrap around you. And, yes, like in the fictional bar Cheers on the TV show of the same name, people actually get to know your name, and your "usual," and can turn a phrase or two with direct eye contact. Gritty's mug club is testament to the hordes of people who call this bar their "local."

This was a Monday where we all sipped pint glasses of water with lunch. It wasn't "beer-thirty" for me, as I had to drive home to Waterville afterward, nor for Richard or Ed, who actually work to run their business, even though they bill themselves in their commercials as "just a couple of guys who are really into beer." There's a time and place for everything, and in that special third place, if you want water, water it is.

We talked a lot about the current state of affairs in the local beer scene, and the influx of nanobreweries in Maine and the rest of New England that make enough beer to sell out of their taprooms or tasting rooms, but don't serve food. "We have to deal with issues like the Americans with Disabilities Act," Richard said, between bites of his sandwich, "making our pubs wheelchair accessible. We pay sales tax and comply with other rules, like replacing a three-bay sink behind the bar with a four-bay sink. We have both breweries and restaurants to run, not just a tiny brewing system and a tasting room."

Ed nods in agreement. "People come in and ask what we have that's new in the way of beer. I tell them that we made 20 different beers just for this Portland pub last year. But we don't make trendy, flavor-profiled beer."

I asked, "What about pumpkin?" I had heard that pumpkin ale accounts for a huge portion of the sales for some regional breweries.

Richard laughs. "We've had a Halloween Ale for 25 years, but there has never been pumpkin in it and there never will be."

"It's an ESB," Ed says, "a traditional extra special bitter."

"We've been here for 25 years," Richard concludes, "and that's a good thing."

Hidden Cove Brewing Company

73 Mile Road
Wells, ME 04090-4135
(207) 646-0228
www.hiddencovebrewingcompany.com

Hidden Cove's taproom is seasonal, so check their Facebook page to make sure they're up and running. In season, enjoy the taproom seven days a week. At other times during the year, you can catch Richard and Sherri Varano pouring their beers for eager crowds at events like the Newport Brew Fest in Rhode Island and a mini-brewfest at Shubie's Marketplace Wine and Spirits in Marblehead, Massachusetts. The beers are also available at select locations in Maine, Rhode Island, and Massachusetts. Check the website for those stores.

Here's the brewer's description of their IPA, called Patroon (6% ABV): "Intense aromas of tropical fruit, melon and orange with subtle hints of pineapple, grapefruit and pine." And when the warm weather finally arrives, try brewer Kevin Glessing's Summer Ale (4% ABV), a session ale made with Meyer lemon and honey.

Wells isn't that far a drive from Boston, so take a dogleg up to Maine on your next trip to the Hub.

Kennebec River Brewery

1771 US 201
West Forks, ME 04985-0100
(800) 765-7238
www.northernoutdoors.com

Ensconced within this popular outdoor resort, Kennebec River Brewery has been operating since the mid-nineties. Stay at the resort, which looks like an old-fashioned and elegant lodge, and do some whitewater rafting, cross-country skiing, or any number of other outdoor activities. Pick your sport, or stay in and read by the fire. Jim Yearwood still makes the beer and, frankly, having a brewpub right on the premises makes for cozy evenings by the fire. *Travel + Leisure* magazine recently included KRB in a list of the countries coolest breweries. Family-friendly fun awaits, and the beer will welcome you back.

If you can't make it to The Forks, Jim travels with his beer to several brewfests each year. Some of his beers are Let 'Er Drift Summer Ale, Sledhead Red, and Magic Hole IPA (available on tap and as six-packs in select New England stores), in addition to rotating beers such as Deer-in-the-Head Lite, Whitewater Wheat, Kennebec Logger, Big Mama Blueberry Ale, Octoberfest, Arthur's Hazelnut Brown, Penobscot Porter, and Class V Stout.

Kennebunkport Brewery / Federal Jack's

8 Western Avenue, Suite 6
Kennebunk, ME 04043-7756
(207) 967-4311
www.federaljacks.com

That was then: Located in the slim area of the Kennebunks known as "Taint Town" (because according to local lore, the land "'taint Kennebunk and 'taint Kennebunkport"), Federal Jack's brewpub was the first place to serve Shipyard beers. It was called Kennebunkport Brewing Company then and had its humble beginnings as a seven-barrel Peter Austin brewing system. Helping Fred Forsley and brewmaster Alan Puglsey install the equipment were Ed Stebbins and Richard Pfeffer of Gritty McDuff's. Since its opening in 1992, "KBC," as it was fondly called, expanded to include Shipyard Brewing Company's huge brewery in Portland, then was returned to the Forsley/Pugsley fold after Miller Brewing Company bought into Shipyard. Through the metamorphosis, however confusing, KBC has retained its seven-barrel charm and waits for you to tour. Then head upstairs to Federal Jack's.

This is now: It's still Kennebunkport Brewing Company, and it still has that same Peter Austin system and the seven-barrel charm. Mike Haley is head brewer, and he concocts a dozen beers a year, each with his signature. Lucky Taint Town! On my last visit I stayed overnight at an inn up the street and brewed the next day with Mike and his crew. I had dinner at Federal Jack's the night before, and even though it was in the dead of winter, in a town where the faint-of-heart take off to warmer climes, the bar had a good-size crowd of locals enjoying appetizers, pub fare, and the homemade beer.

I had to be at the brewery at 8 a.m., so on a heartbreakingly gorgeous winter's day that clocked in at a mere 8 degrees, I first picked up a gigantic cup of coffee at the local general store and gathering place and headed over to the brewery. "Dress in layers" doesn't even begin to tell you how cold a brewery can be until the mashing-in begins and the steam helps warm things up. I "helped" Mike brew a batch of a highly hopped beer, the name of which escapes me now. I think I was so numb with cold that my mind didn't function until after lunch.

You too can brew for a day as part of Shipyard's "Brewing Vacation," which runs from January to mid-May, when production is at a slower pace. It's a fun way to get an idea of what brewing is all about. You visit the small KBC one day and the gigantic Shipyard Brewing Company facility the next, and the VIP treatment you receive is a welcome respite from the everyday grind. See the Shipyard website (www.shipyard.com) for more information (listing apppears later in this chapter).

Liberal Cup Public House and Brewery

115 Water Street
Hallowell, ME 04347-1357
(207) 623-2739
www.theliberalcup.com

Geoff Houghton spoke with me about both of his pubs in 2014. He also owns Run of the Mill in Saco, Maine. See that listing for more of the interview with Geoff.

I live close to the Liberal Cup, and I can attest to its warm, wood-paneled classic pub feel. It's great to have a place like this in central Maine, which can be a wasteland of big-box chain restaurants and fast-food places. The chefs use as many local ingredients as they can find.

Geoff told me, "I opened the Liberal Cup in 2000, realizing a lifelong dream of establishing a traditional English pub on this side of the Atlantic. At the impressionable age of 17, I had fallen in love with the English country pub—a place for families and friends to gather for all occasions, as well as a local watering hole for those out and about or on their way home. English pubs are cozy, informal, and meant for all to enjoy. I hope that is what you'll experience when you walk through our door. It's certainly cheaper than a trip to England, and the food is better. I promise. As for the beers I brew, although I love experimentation, I keep them all within the English tradition: drinkable, affordable, and for the people."

Liberty Craft Brewing

7 Coon Mountain Lane
Liberty, ME 04949
(207) 322-7663
www.libertycraftbrewing.com

Guy Hews just doesn't have enough to do. Not only does he work full-time inspecting bridges as an engineer for the state of Maine, he recently turned a longtime hobby of home brewing into an official business. "I home-brewed for six years and built a structure on my land just for that hobby," Guy says. "It has a wood-fired, 98 percent efficient gasification furnace that Efficiency Maine installed. The upstairs of the building is a tasting room with a beautiful view of the Camden Hills. It's very rustic and looks like a lodge. My friends kept asking me if they could buy my beer, so I made it official and got all the licensing to open a nanobrewery."

Hews is from a long line of blueberry farmers and still rakes enough berries to make a blueberry ale. "I'm named for my great-great grandfather," he says, "and he came down from Canada to farm here. My uncle still owns a lot of the land, which he leases out to other farmers. But there's a family patch and that's where I get my berries."

Located about a mile and a half from the famous Liberty Tool Company (Got Junk?) and Liberty Graphics, Guy's new brewery is a nice addition to a drive in the country. "We won't have food for now," he says. "I didn't want to get licensed as a brewpub." But people have let him know they'd be able to provide food, and that may come to pass. Meantime, feel free to BYOF.

Bottles and growler fills are available of Haystack Pale Ale, Saint George Pilsner, Queen Bee Honey Lager, and Chupacabra Extract IPA, with more to come.

Liquid Riot Bottling Company

250 Commercial Street
Portland, ME 04101-4034
(207) 221-8889
www.liquidriot.com

E-mail tag . . . phone tag . . . but I finally got hold of Eric Michaud, who tells me Liquid Riot has been open since March 2013. His beer bar, Novare Res, opened in May 2008. "I started working at a brewpub working security, did home brewing, traveled around the world studying in Japan, Belgium Trappist monasteries, Italy to check out vineyards, Germany, UK, all the beer-drinking cultures. My wife and I spent a long time abroad. I got into bar management in western Massachusetts. When the time was right, I decided to move back to Maine, where we could raise our child.

"After I opened Novare Res, I decided to open a second place to create my own stuff. So at Liquid Riot we're making some of the best beers in the world. I'm informed by a mix of brewing traditions. I've become friends with some of the best brewers in Europe, and I pick and choose styles. We can brew American-style single infusion, but we can do temperature steps, heat the mash in stages. Belgian brewers do that. We can do a German style of decoction, taking some of the mash out, boiling it, reintroducing it to main mash, upgrading the temperature of the mash. It brings out nuances from the malts and changes the structures of the malts. I do as much as I can of the brewing, and my head brewer is Greg Abbot and assistant brewer is Russell Hoskins. In the distillery, my brother Ian runs the still."

All the food is made in-house, even the charcuterie, with Chef Noly Lopez sourcing local, organic, naturally raised products. Michaud describes the menu as upscale pub, with the chefs having some fun with Asian-influenced items. "We bake all our own bread, make sauces, cure charcuterie," he said. "You can watch it being made: They'll grind locally grown beef, bake bread, brew the beer, make the spirits. You can watch it all being done. We even squeeze out our own soda syrups, bitters and juices."

In 2016 Liquid Riot announced that Nick Krunkkala will take over as executive chef. One of his new dishes is described this way: "Damariscotta River mussels in Liquid Riot's house IPA with wild ramp butter, spring onion, and sweet carrot romesco." I can attest to the quality and flavor of our very own Damariscotta mussels (and oysters, too), so welcome Chef Nick to the Portland food and drink scene. And in the beer department, they released Straight to Black:Out, "a bold and rich Russian Imperial Stout. We aged two batches, one in a bourbon barrel and one in a port wine barrel, to display the effects that types of barrels can have on beer."

Voted the best brewpub in Maine by *RateBeer* in 2013 and 2014, this is a must-visit on any tour of the Portland dining and drinking scene.

Maine Beer Company

525 US 1
Freeport, ME 04032-7009
(207) 221-3159
www.mainebeercompany.com

Whenever Maine Beer Company debuts a new beer, or a fresh batch of an older, beloved brew, there are lines out the door and around the huge brewery. On one premiere day, the beer was "Dinner," and the temperature was, well, bone-chilling. That did not deter the hordes, however. There were even detailed instructions from MBC on how and where to queue up and how much visitors could buy. This is a company with a vision that hit the bull's-eye. Their tasting room is cozy and overlooks the gigantic brewery floor below. No need for a tour—you've got a view to die for, if you like gleaming vessels and sparkling-clean spaces. This is worth the trip to Freeport, folks.

I love their stout, Mean Old Tom (6.5% ABV), and even made meatballs with it. You don't want too much beer in there, just enough to give the sauce a nuance that without the brew it wouldn't have. Here's the story and brewer's description of this mean-tasting stout:

> *Our American-style stout aged on organic vanilla beans. Intense notes of coffee and dark chocolate lead way to subtle notes of natural vanilla. Flaked oats generate a silky mouthfeel.*
>
> *I think it was the summer of '76, I was 5 years old and my uncle Tom came to paint our house. It was in the tiny town of Louisiana, Missouri, on the mighty Mississippi River, where he would take me to stroll the roadside ditches to gather one man's junk (beer cans). In honor of his magnificent treasure (his beer can collection) and his spirit for fast cars, tough motorcycles and mean smiles, we bring you Mean Old Tom.*

Monhegan Brewing Company

1 Boody Lane
Monhegan, ME 04852
(207) 975-3958
www.monheganbrewing.com

Dave Brodrick, founder of Blind Tiger Ale House in New York City, contributed his two cents to an article for First We Feast (www.firstwe feast.com) about bucket-list breweries:

You can't drive to Monhegan—you can only get there by boat, which was how all their brewing tanks arrived. Imagine building a seven-barrel brewery on the backside of an island with 60 year-round residents. All of their ingredients, and most of their customers, arrive by sea during the warmer months (Monhegan is only open from May through October, for obvious reasons). The brewer is Danny McGovern, who's been brewing at various Maine locations for 20 years. For this venture, he partnered up with his daughter and son-in-law. Danny is known for his IPAs and big stouts, which taste pretty good with a fresh island breeze.

I remember Dan McGovern when he was brewing at Belfast Bay Brewing in Belfast, Maine. His oatmeal stout is still being made there, and it's a hugely popular beer, even after two decades.

Norway Brewing Company
237 Main Street
Norway, ME 04268
(207) 739-2126
www.norwaybrewing.com

Opened in April 2016, Norway Brewing is the brainchild of Charlie Magne Melhus and his wife, Erika. I spoke with Charlie right after he had the brewpub's soft opening. Talking about the food end of the operation, he told me, "Right now we have a couple of small plates, a cheese board, some sandwiches, a burger, and we're working on getting some weekly specials on the menu." I think it'll be worth the trip just to try the hand-cut Belgian fries. All the meat is local, as well as the greens and potatoes. Whatever they can get locally, they do. Charlie will always be the executive chef but will have more people in the kitchen as the need arises.

Charlie is also doing the brewing, helped out by his mom and wife. "It's going to be 'the me show' for a while." Speaking of the beers, Norway is still young enough to be creating its lineup. The Green Machine session ale, Left Turn pale ale, and Mr. Grumpypants stout will be among the many, I'm sure, beers that Charlie and his gang will bring to life in the Norway brewery.

Oak Pond Brewing Company
101 Oak Pond Road
Skowhegan, ME 04976-4602
(207) 474-3233
www.oakpondbrewery.com

Mother-and-son team Nancy and Adam Chandler (no, not the Adam Chandler of *All My Children* fame) run this hidden-away, rustic brewery, turning out some really tasty beer. There are some brewers who crave the limelight, but Nancy and Adam do not, although they're certainly worthy of it.

Here's their description of the Oktoberfest: "Oktoberfest is a complex, malty, bottom fermented lager. It has a wealth of flavor and a slightly caramel character. Hops are used sparingly so as to provide balance to its clean personality. Aging for over five weeks gives this lager a round smooth taste. Oktoberfest is an American term for a German beer style and is meant to be enjoyed year round."

Skowhegan is now the home of two craft breweries, so it's worth the trip to visit both Oak Pond Brewing and Bigelow, stopping for lunch at The Pickup Cafe downtown. Oh, and don't forget dessert: The Bankery is a bakery located in a former bank, also downtown. Beer, lunch, dessert—need I say more? This area of Maine sorely needed these types of entrepreneurial spirits, and we finally have them!

Orono Brewing Company
20 Main Street
Orono, ME 04473
(207) 991-7064
www.oronobrewing.com

Owner and brewer Asa Marsh-Sachs—raised on a Maine farm and used to hard, honest work—makes beers such as the beloved Ozone IPA. Here's the brewer's description of the beer named "Winner of 2015 Tap Into Summer Beer Festival that Facebook fans were clamoring for: The Galaxy hop shines here. A light malt body allows the awesome hop flavor and aroma to star. Mosaic and Topaz in the whirlpool, with a huge dry-hopped dose of Galaxy and Mosaic. Big citrus and tropical flavors with lots of resiny hop character as well."

The taproom is open seven days a week, so trek up to this beautiful college town, home of the University of Maine at Orono, and enjoy Asa's brews and some light fare like homemade mac and cheese, flatbreads, and soft pretzels. In the warmer weather, move out to the patio.

Oxbow Brewing Company

274 Jones Woods Road
Newcastle, ME 04553-3123
(207) 351-5962
www.oxbowbeer.com

When I talked with Tim Adams of Oxbow, he had just returned from a trip to Europe. Basking on some beach on the Mediterranean? Hardly. Adams trekked to Italy and Spain at the behest of the Shelton Brothers, importers and exporters of great beer. "We were contacted by the Shelton Brothers to have our beer exported," he explained. "They're from Belchertown, Massachusetts, one of the premier importers of international beer to the US, and they're teaming up with small American craft breweries to do some exporting. They're well-connected in Europe, and we followed their lead on the best markets. There are three main bars featuring our beer. In Rome, Oxbow is at Ma Che Siete Venuti a Fà, known as best beer bar in Italy. In Barcelona, it's at Biercab, and in Copenhagen, the Mikkeller Bar. I went to launch the beer, shake hands, meet the brewer. The publicans themselves can buy direct from importers, and they have warehouses where they store it. It was my first trip to those countries. I was really, really psyched and blown away by the people, food, and beers."

When I asked if beer paired well with pasta, Tim replied, "Certainly. It depends on the dish and the beer, but many of our saisons have dryness, gentle acidity, and hop character that cut through the fattier notes."

Oxbow's flagship is the Farmhouse Pale Ale (6% ABV), which they describe simply as "a saison brewed with American hops." They make many one-offs in what they call their Freestyle Series, and they do some cool collaborations, like Infinite Darkness (11.5% ABV), "an imperial stout brewed in collaboration with our friends at In'finiti Fermentation & Distillation and aged in apple brandy barrels."

Pennesseewassec Brewing
458 Plains Road
Harrison, ME 04040-3829
(207) 743-9808
www.pennybrew.com

Lee Margolin doesn't need a PhD to make beer, he just happened to have one when he started up this impossible-to-spell brewery on the banks of the Crooked River. Margolin brews in a converted in-law apartment. ("No, your mother can't come live with us . . . I'm brewing beer in there!" What a great excuse.) Seriously, though, the beer's excellence is attributed to the water. As Margolin told *Portland Press Herald* columnist Tom Atwell, "The aquifer for that well is in an old glacial moraine that is basically sand or outsize boulders. If we expand or move to a more commercial space, we will still use that water and truck it to the new space."

Pennesseewassee Pale Ale, their take on a traditional English pale ale that is naturally carbonated, is their flagship beer, but others are slated to be brewed. The website doesn't have a beer finder tool, so call the company to see where you can find them. Or check Facebook.

Penobscot Bay Brewery
279 South Main Street
Winterport, ME 04496-0405
(207) 223-4500
www.winterportwinery.com/brewery.asp

Owners Michael and Joan Anderson and family want to meet you. This is a beautiful facility right in town (an albeit tiny town), where Michael brews and the rest of the family are the deckhands. Andy Hazen's son Ben, of Andy's Brew Pub fame, married into the family, so now you have two Maine brewing icons sharing a family tree. Opened in 2001, the business started with a Christmas gift: a wine-making kit that Michael received over 30 years ago.

Here's the description of their newest beer, Mountain Man Double IPA: "Mountain Man, first brewed to celebrate the second anniversary of Nocturnem Drafthaus in Bangor, is an American Double India Pale Ale that an experienced beer drinker will love. Intensely hoppy at 100+ IBUs. Made with Warrior, Centennial, and local Cascade hops. Drinks clean with notes of citrus, pine and earth yet nicely balanced with a smooth, rich malt backbone. Best to drink this one cold and young."

And just when you thought this place had it all (they have a nice gallery where they sell Maine-made crafts), you discover that they make ice cream with a couple of their beers, Half Moon Stout and Black & Tan. Beer, wine, and ice cream: the new food pyramid.

Portland Blending and Bottling / Oxbow Brewing Company
49 Washington Avenue (behind Coffee by Design; do not park in the alley)
Portland, ME 04101
(207) 350 -0025
www.oxbowbeer.com

Surprise! In November 2014 Oxbow made a bold and delightful move and opened a blending and bottling facility with a tasting room in Portland. The beer is still brewed in Newcastle, but their funky and sour beers will be aged here in barrels tanks. For those of you who can't make the trek any farther north than seaside Portland, this is for you. As *Bangor Daily News* culture sleuth Kathleen Deely Pierce reported on November 7, 2014:

> *Beer lovers (geeks and babes) are equally as thrilled to have another place to sip from the nectar of the Maine-made gods. What's different about Oxbow's tasting room?*

There are more than eight beers, like Space Cowboy (the low-alcohol working man's ale) on draft and bottles of smoky Arboreal and Oxtoberfest, a blend of the past three year's autumn ales, to try and purchase. House beers Domestic and Continental are made with US and European hops accordingly.

General Manager Greg Jasgur, who was hired from D.C.'s Piz-zeria Paradiso to man the venture, is a friendly and knowledge pres-ence behind the copper bar. He'll tell you where the hops came from, how they were dried and whether any animals were harmed in the making of Oxbow's beers (answer is none, though they do keep pigs on a 17-acre farm).

Rising Tide Brewing Company

103 Fox Street
Portland, ME 04101-2539
(207) 370-2337
www.risingtidebrewing.com

Heather and Nathan Sanborn may collectively have the most education unrelated to making beer. But in my experience, any knowledge is added value to one's current undertakings. She's a lawyer, he's a former book designer among other interesting things, and in just a few short years, they've taken their company from the industrial park way out in the Riverton section of Portland to the heart of Bayside, where they have one of the most happening tasting rooms around. Heather was active in efforts to have legislation changed to allow breweries to have staff man their booths at festivals (instead of the prior requisite of manning with volunteers who don't know the beers), and she is an important voice in the Maine Brewers Guild.

Good things are always happening at Rising Tide, where you can begin and end a Maine Brew Bus tour, enjoy their newly remodeled and enlarged tasting room, and partake of any number of rotating food trucks parked outside. They have everything from lobster rolls to shawarma to Japanese cuisine parked out front and ready to dish up a tasty meal to go with your beer. There's live music on Sundays, and always special events. I think I may have to get down there for the Mother's Day beer and chocolate pairing. Rising Tide will also schedule your private tour or event.

My favorite beer? Zephr, their yummy IPA (7.2% ABV), described as "redolent of citrus, apples, and pears, balanced by a touch of caramel. We use malted barley grown by local farmers and add a special blend of Cascade, Centennial, and Calypso hops to create this juicy, hoppy ale."

Rock Harbor Pub & Brewing
416 Main Street
Rockland, ME 04841-3345
(207) 593-7488
www.rockharbor.me

Dan Pease knew nothing about running a restaurant when he bought the one that he now occupies, into which he plunked a small brewery. "I bought the system from the Bull Jaeger guys," he says. "It was on Craigslist." (Bull Jaeger's was one of the Portland breweries that people were sad to see go.)

I visited in the spring, before the tourists crowd Main Street. Once rundown and languishing, Rockland is now thriving and can boast a downtown brewpub among its cafes, coffee shops, and the famous Farnsworth Museum. Dan had a good crowd at the horseshoe bar, enjoying some of the 16 beers they keep on tap. My only regret was not trying the lobster rangoons he urged me to try. Hey, Dan, where's that recipe? Here's the description of their very first brew: "Batch 101: Our first beer ever made at Rock Harbor Brewing Co.! This Saison has a little bite at the first sip due to a fast fermentation, similar to a Belgian Style Beer. Try it with a slice of orange!"

A classic pub, Rock Harbor has live music and televisions, so you can belly up, watch the people walk by, or catch a game.

The Run of the Mill Public House & Brewery
100 Main Street
Saco, ME 04072-3500
(207) 571-9648
www.therunofthemill.net

I caught owner/brewer Geoff Houghton on the road, which is when the busiest of the busy often have the time to talk. I asked him about his background: "My dad's English, and I spent a couple of years drinking British ales back in the '80s. I missed them when I came home. I knew I wanted to open a pub, then someone suggested I brew my own beer. Back in the '80s there were only 40 microbreweries. I wrote them asking to learn how to brew, but ended up returning to England and brewed there for three months at Nethergate in the county of Sussex. We brewed the old English styles, the way they've been doing it forever. I heard of Gritty's, wrote to them, and they needed a brewer in 1989. I was Gritty's first brewer besides Eddie Stebbins. I opened the Liberal Cup [in Hallowell, Maine] in 2000. I do about 25 different styles of beer every year, from stouts to pale ales to lagers, Hefeweizens.

"As far as the food served at both my pubs, everything is made from scratch, with an emphasis on pub food, and it's fresh: salad dressings, beer batter, everything. We are also sourcing locally. We add pizzazz to New England cooking. We have a pot roast simmered in beer for five hours. I like to call it advanced New England cooking in good portions. And our pints are 20 ounces.

"When I opened, it was Bud territory and I got all kinds of grief for not serving Bud. It was tough, and I was accused of being a snob. I made and named Bug Lager in honor of that. At the end of the day, if I drink three or four beers, I want something to go down easy."

Sea Dog Brewing Company–Bangor

26 Front Street
Bangor, ME 04401-6418
(207) 947-8009
www.seadogbrewing.com

Sea Dog first opened in lovely Camden, then added locations in the old Bowdoin Mill in Topsham, by the river in Bangor, and near the Maine Mall in South Portland. The Camden location is no longer there, and it's well known that Shipyard Brewing Company owns the brand. That said, Brooks Matthews is a real-live brewer plying his craft at the Bangor location, and on a visit in the spring of 2014 he gave us the tour. They are still using the same Peter Austin system they began with, and Brooks turns out a wide variety of styles all year long that supply all three places. All of them are roomy and cozy: I've been to all three, and each unique location keeps you from feeling anything "corporate."

The menu is huge and varied, with a big chunk of it focused on pub fare. But there are many, many items for people (like me) who are always trying to stay "light." My favorite is the pan-seared rare ahi tuna salad. Healthy and filling at the same time. The beers? Try one of the originals, Old Gollywobbler Brown Ale or Windjammer Blonde.

Sea Dog Brewing Company–South Portland

125 Western Avenue
South Portland, ME 04106
(207) 871-7000
www.seadogbrewing.com

Can you say "breakfast"? Not many brewpubs serve this meal, so it's a great feature of the "SoPo" location. There are standard eggs/toast/bacon combos, but check out the crab and avocado or lobster Benedicts. And if you're nursing a hangover after a rough Saturday night, you might want to just calm things down with poutine. Read this and weep: "French fries, cheese curds, Sea Dog Brown Ale gravy, topped with two poached eggs."

Head over after a slog through the mall, or stop in for a last brew before catching your plane at the jetport. I had a lunch-size portion of seared ahi tuna lettuce rolls with Sea Dog Stout one chilly winter's day. Yum.

Sea Dog Brewing Company–Topsham

1 Main Street
Topsham, ME 04086
(207) 725-0162
www.seadogbrewing.com

This is my go-to Sea Dog, mostly because I lived in Topsham for several years and went there from the beginning. In good weather there is a huge deck overlooking the Androscoggin River, and a Sunday brunch is fun. Best Bloody Mary I've ever had. It is located inside the old Bowdoin Mill, and you can feel the history and see it preserved in old photographs on the walls.

Sebago Brewing Company–Gorham

29 Elm Street
Gorham, ME 04038
(207) 839-2337
www.sebagobrewing.com

Brewing since 1998, Sebago is a mainstay of Maine's craft breweries and pubs. There are now four locations: Portland, Scarborough, Kennebunk, and Gorham. A request for a phone interview with owner Kai Adams turned into an invitation to Sebago's Hoppy Hour, a post–Labor Day event at the brewery where local hops are stripped, beers are sipped, and burgers are scarfed. Watch their website for this fun harvest-home event.

When I had two kids attending the University of Southern Maine at Gorham, we spent many a memorable time here catching up with and feeding them after my son's soccer games. Located in the old train depot building, this Sebago is cozy and friendly. I highly recommend the steak tip salad with Lake Trout Stout.

Sebago Brewing Company–Kennebunk

65 Portland Road
Kennebunk, ME 04043
(207) 985-9855
www.sebagobrewing.com

This location, at The Shops at Longbank, boasts a brick oven, trivia on Monday evenings, wood-fired pizza, and Sebago's brewskis—what could be more tempting? And Kennebunk is gorgeous.

Sebago Brewing Company—Portland
211 Fore Street
Portland, ME 04101
(207) 775-2337
www.sebagobrewing.com

Located downstairs at the Hampton Inn, this Sebago is sometimes one of the few Old Port places open for a late-night nosh and beer. When my daughter Meg returned from a year in China, we wanted to celebrate her homecoming. Her plane from JFK was very late, and thankfully arrived safely. Checking our cellphones at the time, we all looked at each other and said, "Sebago." This is where we toasted Meg's return with friendly staff who took really good care of us. Cheers for safe travels!

Here's the description for one of the originals, Frye's Leap IPA (6% ABV): "From the American caramel malt, which gives Frye's Leap IPA its golden color, to the unique and intense dry-hopped aroma of pine and grapefruit, this beer is every bit as exciting as its namesake."

Sebago Brewing Company–Scarborough
201 Southborough Drive
Scarborough, ME 04074
(207) 874-2337
www.sebagobrewing.com

Located near the Maine Mall, this Sebago location boasts booths, a custom-made bar, and a fireplace. It has long been a favorite gathering place and is right off I-95, if you happen to be passing through. How about a bacon and cheddar half-pound burger with a cold pint? And if you're gluten-free, they'll wrap that baby in lettuce.

Sheepscot Valley Brewing Company
74 Hollywood Boulevard
Whitefield, ME 04353-3729
(207) 549-5530
www.sheepscotbrewing.com

That was then: Owner/brewer Steve Gorrill has been in business only since 1995, but there is already a strong demand for his product. Among Sheepscot's offerings are Madgoose Belgian Ale; White Rabbit, a Belgian white he offers in the summer; and Highlander Scottish Ale, brewed in fall and winter. Steve will be glad to give you a tour, but if you can't make it inland to Whitefield, try his brews at Three Dollar Dewey's or The Great Lost Bear in Portland. Steve occasionally guest-bartends at some of the Portland tap houses. Call ahead and find out when his next gig is. He'll serve you his beers and tell you all about them.

This is now: Steve still brews some great beers, and Dewey's and The Bear are still open. I saw Steve at the Portland Craft Brew Races at the Portland Expo, where he was recovering from surgery and manning his booth bravely solo.

Steve describes his flagship beer Pemaquid Ale as a traditional Scottish border ale with a full malty flavor and crisp finish. You can get this ale on draft at Shaw's Lobster Wharf in New Harbor, Maine. If you're traveling in that area of coastal Maine (off Damariscotta), you should go to Shaw's for oysters and lobster anyway. It's a working lobster harbor, so there's a free show of the lobstermen and women unloading their catches in the early afternoons. I think I have more photos of this scene than I do of my kids. (Just kidding, Sam, Burke, and Meg!)

The encouraging news is that Steve is now advertising tasting room hours every weekend. If you call the number above, there should be a message saying what the hours are, or check their Facebook page.

Shipyard Brewing Company

86 Newbury Street
Portland, ME 04101-4219
(207) 761-0807
www.shipyard.com

That was then: In 1992, real estate consultant Fred Forsley was hired to come up with some ideas for an ailing retail complex in Kennebunk. His first thought was to convince the owners of Gritty McDuff's Brewpub to open a second site there. They declined, but suggested Fred himself open a brewpub with the help of Alan Pugsley, a consultant for Peter Austin and Partners, a British company that specialized in setting up microbreweries and brewpubs. Puglsey had gotten David Geary started as well as Gritty's, and after some discussion, agreed to work with Forsley to create some winning brews for Federal Jack's Brewpub and Kennebunkport Brewing Company.

So "winning" were Pugsley's brews that the business outgrew the seven-barrel system in Kennebunk. Within two years, Forsley brought Pugsley on as a full partner and brewmaster and was looking up and down the midcoast area for a second brewery location. Enticed to Portland by tax incentives bestowed by the city, Forsley decided on a four-acre site on the waterfront, which, before urban renewal's wrecking ball, had been the birth site of poet Henry Wadsworth Longfellow. After much renovation, Forsley's and Pugsley's new company, Shipyard Brewing Company (SBC), started operations in 1994.

This is now: Shipyard celebrated 20 years in 2014. Ever-expanding is the mantra and model SBC follows. During a trip to Italy, I got a chance to see firsthand how popular American craft beers are there.

From my blog:

Shipyard Brewing Company of Portland, Maine, has begun distributing several of its beers in Italy, and the natives couldn't be happier. I had the chance to not only visit some of the places serving one of Maine's earliest-made beers, but I was escorted around Rome by their distributor's rep, Sandro Maione. When I asked Shipyard brewer Bruce Elam for the names of bars with SBC beer in stock, he got the team working to get me connected with Sandro.

It was my first trip to Rome, and we only had two days there. I wanted to see the sights, but I didn't want to pass up this opportunity to see beer from home being enjoyed in Italy. So Sandro gave us a personal car tour, pointing out the ancient Roman sights as we sped our way through Friday evening traffic. By night, with everything lighted up, Rome is spectacular.

Our first stop was at Shamrock Irish Pub. Everyone loves the Irish, don't we? And there are several Irish pubs in Rome. The owner of Shamrock is Alessandro Buzzi and he said he can't keep Shipyard stocked, it's being requested so often. "I had a full cooler last night, and have only four beers left." We lined up the remaining Monkey Fist IPAs on the bar and got some photos. The bar crew was getting ready for the night's rush, but paused to "monkey" around behind the bar gripping bottles of our beer and grinning sheepishly at being asked to pose.

Haus Garten Bagel Bar: What a weird concept, but it looks like it works: beer bar and bagel bar. Why not cover your bases and sell coffee and bagels during the day and serve up beer at night? A really hip place, with original art on the ceiling (not at all like that of the Sistine Chapel, but just as striking), Haus Garten had some Blue Fin Stout and Shipyard Export on hand. I had an Export, with its crispy bite of flavor, realizing how thirsty all this research was making me.

Roma Beer Company: Modern and sleek, this large bar was buzzing by the time we arrived. We did a quick in and out, seeing that their Friday night rush was about to start. Vincenzo Salerno posed at his bar, a little surprised that he was going to be featured in a blog post. Roma Beer Company was carrying Seadog Raspberry Ale, also a Shipyard product, and the hefty price tag was 28 euros for a six-pack. With Euro at about $1.35, that's $37.80! But this is the land of the Lamborghini, after all.

According to Sandro Maione, Shipyard is selling well in Rome, and includes himself as one of its fans. "I like the hoppy beers," he said. Although I don't speak Italian, and he spoke limited English, his message was loud and clear. Italy could open a great new market for American craft beers.

SoMe Brewing Company
1 York Street, Unit 3
York, ME 03909-1392
(215) 718-3541
www.somebrewingco.com

A "silver linings playbook" situation brought this brewery to fruition. David, the son in this father-and-son team, was a high school teacher who got laid off. The duo had been brewing for quite some time by then, and after looking at the bleak teaching landscape, they decided to open the brewery they had dreamed about for so long.

SoMe's year-round beers include Crystal Persuasion (8% ABV), a double pale ale showcasing Crystal hops, and Whoopie Pie Stout (6% ABV), a milk stout aged on cocoa nibs and vanilla beans. They have a nice, sleek tap/tasting room in the beautiful village of York. Lots of rotating beers are also available when "the brewer's ADD dictates" the styles.

Strong Brewing
7 Old Rope Ferry Road
Sedgwick, ME 03907
(207) 359-8722
www.strongbrewing.com

Mia and Al Strong are the first couple of craft beer on the Blue Hill peninsula, brewing favorites like Localmotive pale ale, The Maineiac double IPA, and Soulpatch Porter. The year 2015 brought a major expansion of their brewing system and renovation to the taproom. In addition, the Strongs partnered with Matt Haskell, owner of Finnback Whalehouse in Bar Harbor, to bring a food element to the brewery. That meant a food truck with a wood-fired oven coming to the brewery to serve locally sourced meats, seafood, and other delights.

Located in the little town of Sedgwick, Strong Brewing is a quick trip from Blue Hill. Fill growlers and chat with the person who makes the beer. The day I visited, Mia was holding down the fort, since her husband and brew partner was working elsewhere that day. Al, like many craft brewers, has to work full-time and brew whenever he can around that. Mia decried the new trend of "killing styles," and we had a great talk about the new "hybrid" beers. I took home some of their flagship Localmotive (with a train as a logo), a California common–style beer that is "a pale and hoppy thirst-quencher made with Maine grown pale malt and generous additions of hops."

Sunday River Brewing Company
29 Sunday River Road
Bethel, ME 04217-0847
(207) 824-4253
www.sundayriverbrewpub.com

Note: The correct Facebook page is Sunday River Brew Pub w/ The Savages.

The Savage family purchased Sunday River in 2014. The brewing is still being done by Stu Mason, celebrating over 25 years there making beers like Sunday River ALT, Black Bear Porter, and Momma Mountain IPA, among others. When I spoke with owner Melissa Savage, she boasted about their baker's gigantic New Orleans–style raised doughnut and traditional New England–style doughnuts. The food menu covers breakfast, too, so get in a hearty one before hitting the slopes.

Sunday River is one of the premier ski mountains in Maine, and the brewpub is located at its base. Having said that, Melissa assured me that there are year-round things to do like hiking and camping, as well as many special events. Check out the Bethel Area Chamber of Commerce website at www.bethelmaine.com for a listing.

Three Tides / Marshall Wharf Brewing Co.
2 Pinchy Lane
Belfast, ME 04915-6835
(207) 338-1707
www.3tides.com

Three Tides is the eatery. Marshall Wharf is the house brewery. Together they make beer-pairing heaven, with at least 17 Marshall Wharf beers on tap and a lovely menu of tapas. Situated right over the water in beautiful Belfast, Marshall Wharf beers have been well regarded, and just plain old *loved*, since the beginning in 2007. The beer is also available in cans or on draft all over Maine.

The beauty of playing e-mail tag with a brewer is that sometimes they respond with a nice, long description of their place, and that is exactly what David Carlson did:

"My wife Sarah owns both properties, which are about 40 feet apart. We have 8 drafts in our brewery store to sample. Either get a 9-ounce pour, or to take home with you in growlers and 16-ounce cans. There are currently 16 draft lines of Marshall Wharf beer at the upstairs bar of Three Tides, and another 8 lines in the [seasonal] Biergarten. At times we are pouring 25+ different MW beers throughout the properties." Marshall Wharf brews over 40 different beers a year. They recently released their Weiss Grip Hefeweizen, a Munich-style Hef, and Bitter Truth, an ESB, on draft and in cans.

David went on: "Sexy Chaos, a vanilla and toasted oak Russian Imperial Stout, is always brewed and released just before Christmas, and then again at Valentine's Day." Sounds like a plan, people. Belfast is a walkable seaside village with small shops, bookstores, and an old-fashioned downtown cinema—lots to do.

Tributary Brewing Company

10 Shapleigh Road
Kittery, ME 03904-1480
(207) 703-0093
www.tributarybrewingcompany.com

When I visited Tod and Galen Mott at their nascent brewery in a small strip mall with the post office as their sole neighbor, it was a warm day in May and workers banged and clanged around us. I used a digital recorder to interview Tod as we walked around, but the noise was a formidable opponent. What I witnessed was the couple's long-held dream of owning their own brewery coming true right before their eyes and mine.

A few months after that visit, Tributary was up and running and turning out Tod's great beer. Starting out at Catamount in Vermont, then

Harpoon after it bought Catamount, and a stint at Portsmouth Brewery, Tod Mott is finally captain of his own ship, making great beer. I can't wait to try the one named after me (not really, but I can dream, can't I?): Kate the Great, a Russian Imperial Stout.

In April 2016 Tributary announced the opening of their deck for the season, toasting the event with Double IPA (7.9% ABV), described as "full malt, hop forward balance," with "Mosaic, Simcoe, Centennial dry hop for a dank, citrus, resinous character." The taproom overlooks the brewing equipment, so saddle up, bring in some food, and sample the beer in a flight or pints, with growlers to go.

Maine Beer Bus Tours

The Growler Bus
34 Broad Street
Bangor, ME 04401
(207) 307-6666
www.thegrowlerbus.com

Owned by Gene Beck, publican of Nocturnem Draft Haus in Bangor, the Growler Bus prowls central Maine breweries, wineries, and distilleries. Check out the Atlantic Adventure, which will drive you down Route 1A, the coastal road, to Bar Harbor Cellars Winery, then on to Atlantic Brewing Company in beautiful Bar Harbor. Lunch is at Mainely Meats BBQ, located right on the Atlantic campus (long walk, that 10 feet, whew!). There are other tours, too, including trips to breweries in Orono and Amherst.

Maine Beer Tours
180 Commercial Street
Portland, ME 04101
(207) 553-0898
www.mainebeertours.com

Mark and Nicole Stevens and their crew offer tours every weekend, each hitting at least three brewing destinations. Since August of 2012, Maine

Beer Tours has offered such forays as the Friday Hoppy Hour, Saturday Wake Up, Saturday Hoppy Hour, and Sunday Sipper tours. Check out their website for all the options. You can even rent the bus for your private party.

The Maine Brew Bus

111 Commercial Street
Portland, ME 04101
(207) 200-9111
www.themainebrewbus.com

The Maine Brew Bus is dedicated to promoting the several dozen local breweries by offering a unique and personal beer tour experience. Zach Poole and his crew take you aboard Lenny the lime-green beer bus and you just sit back and enjoy. They do about eight different tours covering Greater Portland and southern Maine, each hitting different breweries, a distillery, a coffee roaster, and even the kombucha cave at Urban Farm Fermentory.

I had a great tour as a special guest along with beer writer Josh Bernstein. We hit four places, all of which were pouring their beers publicly for the first time. Such an honor and a joy to see Bissell Brothers, Banded Horn, Foundation, and Austin Street all become successful in such a short time. And coming in 2016 are tours in Boston. Check the website for all the details, including a trip to Germany for an Oktoberfest tour. Now how about Ireland? Hmm?

Massachusetts

Yes, I'm a Massachusetts girl, born and raised in apple country, Littleton, which I'm proud to say recently celebrated its 300th birthday! If you go by on Route 495, stop and try Kimball's Farm ice cream. It's the best in the world, I think. I moved to Maine to go to Colby College, then came back permanently in 1989. But I still miss my little town on the Minuteman Trail.

I became cognizant of the existence of beer far before the craft beer movement began. I have a memory of tasting beer, probably a Carling Black Label or Narragansett, when I was 10 years old—that was 1963—when my dad let me have a sip. It was a midsummer day, one of those hot and hazy Saturday afternoons with the insects setting up a steady buzz outside, and the beige plastic radio on the kitchen table crackling with the sounds of Ned Martin's voice and the Red Sox game.

Now for the beer. There are over 115 craft brewers in the Bay State, so get on your walking shoes, because you have a lot of work to do.

3cross Brewing Company
26 Cambridge Street
Worcester, MA 01603
www.3crossbrewing.com

"What happens when you blend a passion for bikes and beer?" That's the tagline of this brewery. And what does the name mean? "3cross refers to the traditional spoke lacing pattern in a bicycle wheel," they say. "Each spoke crosses three other spokes on its trip from the hub to the rim. What can we say? We're bike people."

Dave Howland and his wife, Jess, are getting cyclists and non-cyclists together in a roomy, stellar tasting room to drink great beer and cultivate community in their city of Worcester. One of the beers on tap is Batch #152, a Belgian dark strong ale with notes of toffee, treacle, currants, banana, and black pepper. 3cross doesn't serve food, but they invite you to bring your own or order from local eateries.

Aeronaut Brewing Company
14 Tyler Street
Somerville, MA 02143-3224
(617) 718-0602
www.aeronautbrewing.com

Dan Rassi, Benjamin Holmes, and Ronn Friedlander (who recently earned his PhD in microbiology) are the owners of Aeronaut, and at the time I spoke with Dan, they'd been up and running for three months.

Located in a building that once housed the Ames Safety Envelope Company, Aeronaut shares the enormous factory space with 42 other tenants. In an innovative setting, the guys are making innovative brews. Quickly summarizing what I hear are spectacular beers, Dan says, "We have a huge range of styles running the gamut: wheat, hoppy, stouts, Belgians. Ben and Ronn are MIT students, so we're introducing people to the science of making beer a little bit more than other breweries. We have an extensive yeast lab going on. Our taproom is huge, with the main draw being our events. For example, we had an Oktoberfest here last week with over 1,000 people in attendance and tons of food trucks. We also give full pours and growlers."

Dan continued to list what he believes are the real draws to Aeronaut: "We have relationships with a lot of the people we get ingredients from, such as hop growers Four Star Farms in Northfield. Something else unique is what we call Foods Hub, where local businesses come here to produce or showcase their products." Coffee roaster Barismo and Somerville Chocolate are among those who rent the space—an incubator within a brewery.

Amherst Brewing Company
10 University Drive
Amherst, MA 01002-2243
(413) 253-4400
www.amherstbrewing.com

Founded in 1997, Amherst Brewing Company has undergone several expansions and has settled into its most recent incarnation at 10 University Drive, a former Gold's Gym. The space has been completely renovated, providing plenty of room and free parking, no mean feat in downtown Amherst. They boast awards won for their brews at major beer festivals almost every year from 2002 through 2012, when they took a silver medal in the Great International Beer Festival for a barrel-aged version of Black Friday Russian Imperial Stout.

The menu features lots of pub fare. One particular item caught my eye: Brewer's Meatloaf covered with bacon, served with mashed potatoes and smoked porter onion gravy. On a rainy autumn day, this dish sounded like heaven. ABC is also working on expanding their vegetarian and gluten-free selections. Their list of entertainment and events is huge, and they host interesting guest taps, too. Check them out, and visit the Emily Dickenson house while you're in town.

Backlash Beer Company
Boston, MA 02215
(617) 615-9345
www.backlashbeer.com

Backlash beers and founder Helder Pimentel have garnered a lot of great reviews and lots of press, so give them a try. The beers are brewed contract-style at Paper City Brewing in Holyoke and will also be brewed at Foolproof Brewing in Rhode Island, but Pimentel has brewing chops himself. Going from 22-ounce "bombers" to cans is in his plan for 2106, which will bring him more in line with how things are being done in this competitive industry. They currently distribute throughout Massachusetts.

Try the Groundswell, a Belgian blond ale, and Ricochet, an IPA, among others.

Bad Martha Brewing Company

270 Upper Maine Street
Edgartown, MA 02539
(508) 939-4415
www.badmarthabeer.com

Once brewed by Ipswich Brewing Company, Bad Martha now has its very own brewery and tasting room on the premises. Jim Carleton is doing the brewing honors and keeps 10 beers on tap for visitors' enjoyment. Built by the Amish in Pennsylvania and reassembled on-site, the brand-new facility is classic post-and-beam and it's a beauty.

Among the 20 or so beers Jim makes with local, organic, and sustainably raised ingredients, these four make for happy summer drinking: Martha's Vineyard Ale, Martha's Summer Ale, Island IPA, and Vineyard Honey Ale. The brewery offers cheese plates, charcuterie, and crudités for noshing pleasure.

Barrington Brewery and Restaurant

420 Stockbridge Road
Great Barrington, MA 01230-9512
(413) 528-8282
www.barringtonbrewery.net

Brewing since 1995, the restaurant has been around since 1977 and has garnered many honors, including recommendations in Frommer's travel guides. From the solar-powered brewery, the first on the East Coast, come beers like Berkshire Blonde, Hopland Pale Ale, Barrington Brown, and Black Bear Stout. As I write this, it's counting down to Christmas and the winter menu includes Yule Fuel, Scottish Ale, Extra Special Bitter, and a cask-conditioned Scottish.

As for the food, I can't believe my eyes. The prices are among the most reasonable I've seen for local, local, local-as-you-can-get ingredients. Everything is made from scratch, and they have an on-staff pastry chef. Each day features a special dinner, and if you never get tired of turkey, get yourself down there on Sunday for a roast turkey dinner with all the fixings for $14. Then there's prime rib on Thursdays and, of course, being New England, Fridays are for fried seafood. Wash them all down with a beer or two. Or you could show up on Wednesday and have their burger-and-a-beer special for $10.

Bentley Brewing Company
12 Crane Street
Southbridge, MA 01550-1994
(508) 274-9300
www.bentleybrewing.com

Open two years and counting, Bentley Brewing is the brainchild of own-ers and brewers Adam Golka and Mike Lynch. "We've always wanted a place dedicated to just tastings and growlers," Adam said. "It's an awe-some space to just relax, hang out, and talk beer." The beers and taproom (and the people) get five-star reviews, a testament to talent and just being nice.

Following is a selection of beers recently available: Half Nelson (5.5% ABV), an American pale ale; Full Nelson (7.2% ABV), a rye IPA; Shot in the Dark (6% ABV), an American stout; Fearless Squirrel (4.7% ABV), a nut brown; Parts and Labor (7% ABV), a black IPA; and Joy Ryed (6.5% ABV), a saison-style ale.

Berkley Beer Company
17 Cotley Street
Berkley, MA 02779
www.berkleybeer.com

Berkley is not set up to do tours, and they don't plan on adding tours to their program. Owner and brewer Glenn Barboza called on a Monday in August. "Today is paperwork day, paying the bills. I'm going to do some kegging this afternoon." Glenn explained that he brews in a residential neighborhood, and he doesn't think it's fair to open a tasting room there for his neighbors' sakes.

Nate Byrnes, who blogged for a time at Good Brew Hunting, wrote this piece about Berkley's Coffee Porter just for this book:

Opening a bomber of Berkley's Coffee Porter is like stepping foot in God's own coffee shop . . . one's nostrils are filled with a deep, dark, roasted coffee aroma. To be clear, I mean that top-notch, freshly roasted coffee aroma that can only come from a shop that roasts their own beans, not some national chain.

That coffee aroma is matched by the flavor when the brew hits the tongue. But this is no super-roasted Starbucks—the flavor is perfectly balanced between not-too-sweet and not-too-bitter coffee, the dark, roasted malt flavors that accompany any porter, and hints of chocolate. Coffee is present, of course, but is surprisingly subdued after the aroma's punch-in-the-nose. The delicious flavor disappears from the palate almost immediately, leaving a crisp, cleansed mouth that's ready for another sip.

Like any good porter, the beer is unexpectedly light on the tongue. A crisp, slightly mineral flavor washes across the tongue with nary a footprint left behind. No slickness, no heavy mouthfeel. Some drinkers are surprised by how light it feels and are almost disappointed by the lack of body, but the light texture is intentional. It allows the drinker to have several beers without their palate becoming fatigued.

The brew's 6% ABV is just right for a porter . . . enough to build complexity of flavor, but not so much that it knocks a drinker out.

Berkley Beer's T-shirts read "Waste Not, Want Another." Their Coffee Porter is definitely not a beer to be wasted and is so delicious that the drinker can't help but want another. This may be the ultimate dessert beer, but its lightness makes it a great year-round sipper for any occasion. Sadly, it's only available in the fall/winter, so be sure to stock up.

About Nate Byrnes: Nate has been an amateur brewer for over a decade, and put his passion for beer into a beer column called "Good Brew Hunting," which ran biweekly in the *New Bedford Standard Times* from

March 2013 through November 2014. You can read from the archives at www.goodbrewhunting.com.

Berkshire Brewing Company

12 Railroad Street
South Deerfield, MA 01373-0251
(413) 665-6600
www.berkshirebrewingcompany.com

Twenty years after Chris Lalli and Gary Bogoff decided to open a brewery in western Massachusetts, Berkshire Brewing has grown exponentially from a conceived draft-only brewery to a regional brewery producing over 17,000 gallons of beer a week that is available in five states. Here's the brewer's description of the beer that started it all, Steel Rail Extra Pale Ale (5.3% ABV): "BBC's flagship brew is a light colored, medium bodied ale exhibiting exceptional freshness through its 2-Row Pale malt backbone and signature hop flavor and aroma. In the words of renowned beer writer Lew Bryson, Steel Rail EPA is 'what the water in heaven oughta taste like.'"

Amherst and Northampton are not too far away if you want to grab a bite before or after the 1 p.m. Saturday tour.

Big Elm Brewing

65 Silver Street
Sheffield, MA 01257-9626
(413) 229-2348
www.bigelmbrewery.com

Christine and Bill Heaton met and fell in love while working at Victory Brewing in Downington, Pennsylvania. Over time and through obstacles, the couple eventually decided to open Big Elm in Sheffield. With the Heatons' combined brewing experience (after Victory, they owned Pittsfield Brew Works), they have truly found "home." Stop by for six-packs of cans, growlers, or bombers.

Here's the brewer's description of 413 Farmhouse Ale (6% ABV): "This rustic, golden ale is . . . brewed with choice barley, wheat malt, and local honey from Bear Meadow Apiary. We also add a little love in the kettle with whole flower chamomile, lemon zest, and Brazilian pink peppercorn from HimalaSalt in Sheffield."

Blue Hills Brewery

1020 Turnpike Street
Canton, MA 02021-2823
(781) 821-2337
www.bluehillsbrewery.com

Andris Veidis and Peter Augis teamed up to bring you Blue Hills beers, with the tagline "Take the Hill!" Their flagship is Blue Hill IPA, described as having "a fiery amber color and a note of citrus stemming from the American Summit and Golding hops. At 6.6% ABV / 72 IBU, this is a tasty ale with an approachability rarely found in other East Coast IPAs." They also offer Tree Beer, a Kölsch made in collaboration with the local rock band Tree, and made a pineapple wheat beer for Cinco de Mayo.

Blue Hills has a growler club: Buy 10, get the 11th free (well, 5 cents). Check the website for the current beer lineup, where to find them, and events like this one that cracked me up: "Bottoms Up Yoga and Brewery Tour. Yoga: Because punching people is frowned upon. Beer: Because beer."

Bog Iron Brewing Company

33 West Main Street, Unit F
Norton, MA 02766-2711
(508) 952-0555
www.bogironbrewing.com

Bog Iron's third anniversary was on New Year's Day 2016, and owners and brewers Matt Menard, Frank White, and Brian Shurtleff had much to celebrate.

The story behind the brewery's name is an interesting one, according to Brian: "Frank was looking through some old pictures in the online archives of a certain college that is located about 200 yards from us, and he came across a picture of an iron foundry that was built right down the road from us (it is still there), I believe in the early 1700s. What did they smelt in this foundry? You guessed it, 'bog iron.' It was apparently dredged from the local lakes, ponds, and bogs. Out of what felt like 4.5 million possible names, Frank and Matt loved 'Bog Iron.' While Brian whined and moaned (I still don't like the name), Matt and Frank out-voted him and Bog Iron Brewing was born."

The taproom opened in August 2014, so you can now visit and taste the beers, which are brewed on a 3 bbl system. They offer full 16-ounce pours, 4-ounce pours, flights of four, and 2-ounce samples of whatever they are pouring that day. One fan said Bog Iron was his "happy place" and that no matter what beers they have on tap, they are all amazing. Well said. It's pretty mandatory to check their Facebook page to see the daily list, and sometimes there are surprises: The day I checked in with them, they were offering Jump Back, an American IPA in 22-ounce bottles, a rare treat.

Boston Beer Company / Samuel Adams

30 Germania Street
Boston, MA 02130-2312
(617) 368-5000
www.samueladams.com

There's no question that Sam Adams is not technically a craft brewery, but the tours are popular and, like the big breweries elsewhere in New England, offer something for anyone over age 21. For instance, the Morning Mash-In Tour. Up early? Get thee to mashing-in, the first step in brewing, where the brewery fills up with warm steam and the aroma of steeping grains fills your nostrils. I'd have a big ol' Starbucks with me that early. See the website for tour times and for very detailed information regarding parking, ID requirements for sampling the beer, arrival times, and the beers available in growlers.

The Brewmaster's Tavern

4 Main Street (GPS: 2 Petticoat Hill Road)
Williamsburg, MA 01096
(413) 268-7741
www.thebrewmasterstavern.com

From 1812 to the present, this building has been home to taverns and inns, a store, and a livery. Today Brewmaster's is the restaurant, while Opa Opa Brewing (later in this chapter) makes beer in a big building out back. As brewer Mike Charpentier explains, Opa Opa started in 2004 in Southampton and outgrew its brewing space there. They make some specialty brews that are served only in the brewpub. Here, in their words, are two of the many old-fashioned "rules" for the pub:

13th "Drink not nor talk with your mouth full neither Gaze about you while you are a Drinking."

14th "Drink not too leisurely nor yet too hastily. Before and after Drinking wipe your Lips breath not then or Ever with too Great a Noise, for it's uncivil."

The menu is varied, with everything from pub fare to pizza to pasta and classic New England dishes like pot roast and turkey dinner, steaks, and burgers. You name it, even a "lighter fare" menu.

Building 8 Brewing

320 Riverside Drive
Northampton, MA 01060
(413) 250-1602

Building 8 IPA, the flagship brew, has made a big splash in western Massachusetts, garnering praise from fans on Facebook and even receiving an "outstanding" rating (92 score) on *BeerAdvocate*'s website. Brewer Mike Yates, formerly at Amherst Brewing, makes this West Coast–style, hop-forward IPA. They often run out of this popular beer, so be sure to check their Facebook page before heading out.

Buzzards Bay Brewing Company
98 Horseneck Road
Westport, MA 02790-1328
(508) 636-2288
www.buzzardsbrew.com

Boasting of the high quality of their water, Buzzards Bay Brewing, or BBB as they refer to themselves, surely does have a leg up on some areas where beer is brewed. Water can be tinkered with to get it just right for great-tasting beer, but there's something poetic about having your very own water-from-the-farm to work with. Here's the lineup of beers, and be mindful that they, like most craft brewers worth their salt, have more "in the queue": Buzzards Bay IPA, Moby D, tHeGoLdeNfLoUnder, and Swamp Yankee IPA. There's a lot of fun to be had here, with live music in the taproom as well as soup, sometimes a clambake, fire pits outside when the weather is conducive, and a vineyard and winery nearby.

Cambridge Brewing Co.
1 Kendall Square, Building 100
Cambridge, MA 02139-1592
(617) 494-1994
www.cambridgebrewingcompany.com

That was then: CBC's beers have pleased the palates of Cantabrigians as well as garnering more official notice: The brewery's Belgian Tripel won the 1992 Great American Beer Festival gold medal in the specialty-ale category, and its Charles River Porter took the 1990 bronze in the porter group.

This is now: Yes, CBC is still there, and in 2014 celebrated 25 years! They are still winning awards, and their amazing food is locally sourced and thoughtfully prepared and presented. I was lucky to have brewmaster Will Meyers all to myself back then, on the chilly day I walked all over Boston and Cambridge to visit as many breweries and brewpubs as I could. Afterward, at Will's suggestion, I bought the "Three Tenors" CD and wore it out listening to Pavarotti and his friends shatter the chandelier with their beautiful operatic voices.

There's a new mural to see, installed in November 2014, by local artist Liz LeManche, which shows many local and national celebs enjoying a brew. The beers are still impeccable. In Will's words:

Our house beers are all flavor-forward using only water, malt, hops, and yeast. Their profiles of caramel notes, hops, light malt, and roast, respectively, offer something for everyone according to their tastes. Our single-batch beers and seasonals allow us greater range of ingredients, processes, and creative freedoms as we strive to authentically re-create many historical beer styles from around the world. Whether we are brewing a simple classic pilsner, an unhopped herbal gruit beer, or more obscure styles such as Polish grätzer, we want to succeed in presenting a beer true to its roots.

The food? Still delectable. Here's an item from the menu that caught my eye on a cold, gray winter's day: Duck Cassoulet, consisting of duck breast, pork belly, garlic sausage, Maine heirloom beans, and parsley crumb.

I caught Will Meyers on his way up to Vermont as he was heading to The Alchemist, then to see Paul Taylor at Zero Gravity, "moving some hops around the country." I asked about the sake/beer hybrid Will makes once a year. The process is pretty complicated, but the result sounds like it's worth the trip to Cambridge to sip one.

When I asked Will how he keeps things interesting after 22 years there, he said:

It's always interesting. We have so many great people at CBC, we're always defining our craft with traditional expressions of beer, and at the same time we're experimenting. We've branched out into bottling and canning the beer, which has been something new for me. [After nearly a quarter-century of customers asking, CBC finally decided to break their draft-only model and package some of the beers.] Phil [Bannatyne] and I have had a tremendous partnership for going into our third decade. Our beers are available throughout New England.

And we enjoy seeing many of our former brewers heading out to open their own breweries.

Cape Ann Brewing Company

11 Rogers Street
Gloucester, MA 01930-5014
(978) 282-7399
www.capeannbrewing.com

Consistent winner of a "Best of the North Shore" award, Cape Ann Brewing is right on the Gloucester waterfront. They are proud of their beers, which they typify as: "Fisherman's beer—whose bold flavor and character reflect the spirit and courage of the sailors of the North Atlantic fishing fleet—is a tribute to hard work and a salute to friendships that endure."

If you're on the water, you've got to try an Oyster Stout (5.3% ABV), one of at least a dozen brews available at any given time. Here's the brewer's description: "Using hundreds of crushed oyster shells in our mash, the result is a roasty stout with a rich body and smooth mouth-feel to go with its unique flavor and aroma."

There is a nice selection of food, baked and fried of what else but seafood. But that's not all. In addition to haddock, scallops, shrimp, clams, and calamari, there are sandwiches, pork belly confit, lobster mac and cheese, and lots of soups, salads, and small plates.

Cape Cod Beer

1336 Phinneys Lane, Suite 2-2
Hyannis, MA 02601-1875
(508) 790-4200
www.capecodbeer.com

Now more than 10 years strong, Cape Cod Beer announced at the end of 2014 that they'd won six medals at the Great International Beer and Cider Festival. Here's the booty they brought back: gold for Cape Cod Weizenbock, Cape Cod Harvest Ale, and Christmas in July; bronze for Cape Cod Dunkelweizen, Cape Cod IPA, and Kurt's Farmhouse Ale.

What's happening in the taproom? Event central. Check these out: a hula hoop class with a pint of beer afterward; "yappy" hour—bring your dog and have a beer; and an event called "Glued," a craft night where you enjoy beer and take home your beachy creation. For summer Cape Cod Beer released Hot Blonde, an American golden ale aged on poblano, serrano, and jalapeño peppers and described as having "lots of great pepper flavor and a touch of heat."

Castle Island Brewing Company

31 Astor Avenue
Norwood, MA 02062
(781) 951-2029
www.castleislandbeer.com

Adam Romanow answered some questions for me about his brewery before its opening in December 2015:

> **Kate:** What will inform your beer styles?
>
> **Adam:** Our beers are inspired by local flavors, traditions, and attitudes. By drawing on Boston's robust, diverse past and present, we'll be exploring styles across the board. That said, I'm a certified hophead, and we plan to have at least one IPA available at all times.
>
> **K:** What is your favorite food paired with what beer?
>
> **A:** I'm a big seafood guy—"moules frites" with De Ranke XX Bitter is a classic pairing, but I also love a lobster roll from Sully's (at Castle Island) with something local and hoppy, like Trillium Fort Point Pale Ale. And there's something so comforting about a Fenway Frank and a cold Bud Light when you're at a Sox game. I know I'll get crap for that last one, but tradition is tradition.

When I checked in with Castle Island again, I learned that, true to his word, Adam turned out a winning IPA, Candlepin, which was cited by Thrillist's Zach Mack as a "Best Canned Craft Beer for Your Cooler Right Now" (www.thrillist.com). Mack, a certified Cicerone and owner of Alphabet City Beer Co. in New York City, said Candlepin is "everything you'd want a session beer to be."

Cisco Brewers
5 Bartlett Farm Road
Nantucket, MA 02584-2928
(508) 325-5929
www.ciscobrewers.com

There once was a place called Nantucket . . . Oh holy trinity of imbibers everywhere, Cisco is the site of a brewery, a winery, and a distillery. Once you get the ferry over, why leave? Cisco Brewers, Nantucket Vineyard, and Triple Eight Distillery, period.

Read Cisco Brewers' intriguing and humorous history on their website. The brewery's humble beginnings (think no room at the inn) were outside, as in outdoors. Weather? Of course, all kinds of weather. But eventually they got a proper building, which you can visit year-round. In addition to their "classic" beers, such as Whale's Tail Pale Ale, Cisco makes many other styles and seasonals; for example, Winter Shredder (8.8% ABV), a braggot, which is a mead made with malt.

Clown Shoes Beers
55 Mass Avenue
Lexington, MA 02420-4001
(781) 365-1137
www.clownshoesbeer.com

Clown Shoes is brewed at Ipswich Ales, and the beers are available in roughly half of the 50 states, according to their beer finder. They have a lot of fans and got a ranking in the top 100 beers by *RateBeer* in 2014. In 2016 they released an election-cycle beer called Third Party Candidate, described by Gregg Berman on their blog as "an Imperial Pale Lager, dry hopped heavily with Idaho 7, Sterling, and Columbus." I watched a very good review on YouTube by The Mighty Plantain of Clown Shoes' 2016 release of Luchador En Fuego, a Bourbon-barrel-aged stout spiced with vanilla and ancho and chipotle peppers.

Element Brewing Company
16 Bridge Street
Millers Falls, MA 01349-1334
(413) 835-6340
www.elementbeer.com

Owners and brewers Ben Anhalt and Dan Kramer celebrated six years of "Art, Science, Beer" in December 2015. Ben rattled off a slew of places the beer is distributed, including Alabama and Australia! The guys had many years' combined experience in the craft beer business when they decided to go out on their own. "We're both from around the area and a contractor friend of ours knew the place was open and rent was cheap, so we jumped right in," Ben said. "We brew four beers year-round and a rotating seasonal, so when they're gone, they're gone. We have different one-offs here and there. All of them are fusions of different styles to make a balanced beer."

One of the brand-new ones being distributed was Dark Vanilla, "dry hopped," Ben chuckled, with Madagascar vanilla beans. "We don't brew to style," he said, which is why I guess they call their product "Element" and not beer. Ben says to check Facebook and Twitter for their updates and event announcements. As this book went to press people were talking about—okay, salivating over—Extra Special Oak, with "notes of vanilla bean and spice with underlying aromas of rich malt. Layers of flavors follow, from toasted coconut to warm bread to green tea."

Exhibit 'A' Brewing Company
81 Morton Street
Framingham, MA 01712
(508) 202-9297
www.exhibit-a-brewing.com

I was chasing down Matthew Steinberg because I wanted to find out about his former brewery, Blatant Beer. Instead, through a series of Facebook messages and a subsequent phone call, I got the scoop from Matt on his new venture, Exhibit 'A' Brewing Company. It's a textbook case of why social media is crucial for brewers. I'm way up here in central Maine, which on a rainy day in May can feel like a distant planet from the world of beer. (Okay, I'm whining. We have almost a dozen craft breweries within an hour of here.)

Now on to Matt's news. First, the location: Exhibit 'A' occupies the former Jack's Abby space. Matt has completely renovated the 12,000-square-foot facility and taproom. "My model for the taproom will be a place for people to come, taste the beer, and take some home. It's cozy and quaint and welcoming, but not meant as a place to hang out for hours." I wonder about the beers. Matt says, "I haven't revealed the beer names yet, but here goes." (I feel like Lois Lane, getting a big scoop!) They'll start with four:

- Goody Two Shoes: Described by Matt as "a traditional, expressive Kölsch, in the authentic style."

- Cat's Meow IPA: "I love the hop-forward movement," Matt said, "and I'm putting my own stamp on what a New England IPA can be. Cat's Meow is a classic 6.5% ABV, on the drier side, with low bitterness and pronounced flavor and aroma."

- Mindset Pale Ale: According to Matt, this is "a kickback to the old days. We'll be using high-oil Cascade hops from Segal Ranch in Washington State by third-generation hop farmer John Segal. These are the best hops on the planet."

- Coffee beers: "I'm working with Andrew Sanni of Barrington Coffee, who is roasting extra light to fairly dark roasts trying to find flavors not found typically. There is a cool relationship between coffee and beer, and we'll unveil those as we get them brewing."

I asked Matt about his brewing background, and he rattled off the places he's worked: three years as head brewer at Offshore, four years at Mayflower, then the stint with Blatant Beer. "But my favorite job so far was the two years I was a stay-at-home parent." We chuckle. Let's toast to priorities!

Gardner Ale House

74 Parker Street
Gardner, MA 01440-3809
(978) 669-0122
www.gardnerale.com

Owner Rick Walton loves to tell the story of how he turned a biology major and an engineering degree into his dream: "My competition is your refrigerator and your TV," he told me the summer after I had come back from a trip to the Bay State to visit brewpubs and had had a really nice lunch at Gardner Ale House. "I want to create a third place. Not home, not work, but a place where everyone knows your name. I want to get people out from behind their iPads and into the pub, where they can be social. I have street parties here to get people together with burgers and beer. Then there is the huge Oktoberfest celebration." He's not kidding. When I got on his website in midsummer, it had a real-time clock ticking down the seconds until October.

Although at first Walton did all the brewing by himself, often working around the clock, he later trained Dave Richardson, a younger neighbor who tagged along at Walton's elbow while he home-brewed. Richardson loved brewing so much, he went to California to get his master brewer's diploma. He now brews over 24 different beers that are served exclusively at the ale house, with 8 to 10 on tap at a time. They have guest taps, too, so you can find what you want. "My beer doesn't go anywhere except over my bar," Walton says. The food? There's a huge menu where every single item is homemade, even the chicken tenders. The day I had lunch there, I had a fabulous salmon steak with miso glaze and sautéed baby bok choy for $10 and shared a sampler with my son.

Check out the website for the full list of beers. Among the many offerings is Abbey Rye (5.7% ABV), described as "a traditional Belgian style Abbey Ale with an untraditional twist of rye. Rye malt accentuates the already spicy and zesty flavors coming from the use of traditional Belgian Ale yeast, and increases the dryness, yet smoothes the mouth feel. Brewed by your local, friendly downstairs 'Monk.'"

Goodfellow's Brewing Company

8 Race Course Road
Lakeville, MA 02347-1826
www.goodfellowsbrewing.com

In a note on the website from owner/brewer John Goodfellow, he outlines how his brewery came to be: "Goodfellow's Brewing Company began . . . when my wife bought me a home brewing 'kit' for $14 at a Massachusetts discount retailer. The beer that came from that kit ultimately went down the drain, but my fascination in the process of creating beer, perfecting my skills as a brewer, and launching Goodfellow's Brewing Company only grew over time."

Customers rave about Goodfellow's WheneverFest Ale (7% ABV). According to the brewer's description, it is "inspired by traditional German fest beers but made as a full-bodied ale and is available—well, whenever! This ale's light hop characteristics and sweet, mild Vienna malt make for a very drinkable beer that finishes cleanly and refreshingly."

When I caught up with John, he gave me a list of his current lineup in addition to the WheneverFest, which is still a fan favorite: Race Course English Pale Ale (7% ABV), The Townsman American Stout (7.5% ABV), Frugal Farmer Golden Ale (6% ABV), South Coast Select Irish Red (6% ABV), South Coast Select Blueberry Wheat (5% ABV), and Dark Maple Scottish Ale (7.5% ABV). Find Goodfellow's beer in pubs and retail shops by using the beer finder toggle on the website.

Harpoon Brewery–Massachusetts

306 Northern Avenue, Suite 2
Boston, MA 02210-2367
(617) 456-2322
www.harpoonbrewery.com

Harpoon is another brewery that has grown beyond "craft" in terms of the amount of beer they brew, but I hear great reviews of their beer hall and their beers. Started by Dan Kenary and Rich Doyle in 1986, they boast

"Brewing Permit #001 in the Commonwealth of Massachusetts because it was the first brewery to commercially brew and bottle beer in Boston in more than 25 years." In 1987 Harpoon Ale was introduced into two Boston pubs. The following year Winter Warmer, which they claim to be the first seasonal beer brewed in New England, surprised drinkers with the tastes of cinnamon and nutmeg. Things have come a long, long way since then. Enjoy a pint and a pretzel in their beer hall, as well as craft brewing history.

Idle Hands Craft Ales
89 Commercial Street
Malden, MA 02148
(617) 819-4353
www.idlehandscraftales.com

Brewing Belgian-inspired beers, Idle Hands is a popular craft brewery. Grab one of their beers, and it will "keep your idle hands from becoming the Devil's workshop."

Opened in 2011 by University of New Hampshire alum Christopher Tkach, the brewery was originally in Everett, Massachusetts. In the spring of 2016 they completed a move to Malden, where they have a taproom and a much-expanded brewing system, from 5 bbl to 15 bbl. Chris told me they'll be getting back into brewing their German lagers, like Klara, which Facebook fans were clamoring for. They'll also do some Brett saisons, among many other of their popular brews. I had to let the busy brewer get back to work, but this is an exciting development. Get down to Malden and try these beers.

Independent Fermentations Brewing
127 Camelot Drive
Plymouth, MA 02360-1422
(508) 789-9940
www.independentfermentations.com

Like many craft brewers who make great beer, Indie Ferm expanded into another unit in their building to keep up with demand. This new space has an event room up front and a large space out back for brewing apparatus. Brewed with 80 percent locally sourced ingredients, the beer is packaged in 22-ounce bombers or in kegs (for restaurants). They self-distribute the beer with a focus on southeastern Massachusetts; check the "sightings" tab on the website for places you can find it.

In 2016 they announced their upcoming beers, among them a name that drew a chuckle, Cloudy With a Chance of Cranberries (9% ABV), available only in the taproom and described as follows: "It started with Honey Tripel and quickly evolved into something else with the addition of local cranberries and more honey. It seems like it also picked up some wild yeast. The result is a cloudy saison-like beer with a dry finish and a hint of cranberry."

Ipswich Ale Brewery
2 Brewery Place
Ipswich, MA 01938-2044
(978) 356-3329
www.ipswichalebrewery.com

That was then: Since its grand opening in October 1992, Ipswich Brewing Company has increased in size thirteen-fold, producing Ipswich Ale, Ipswich Dark Ale, and Ipswich Oatmeal Stout, plus an annual seasonal brew.

This is now: Ipswich is now a regional brewery, making all their venerable beers like Ipswich Winter Ale and their oatmeal stout, all widely distributed. In 2015 Ipswich completed a spectacular expansion of its brewery and added an on-site restaurant called Ipswich Ale Brewer's Table. There are 15 taps of their great beers and a chef in the kitchen who turns out New American cuisine and traditional pub fare. The lobster and bacon sandwich with Gouda sounds pretty amazing. Check their website for a full slate of events, like Mother's Day at the Brewery, tap takeovers, and other community involvement.

And lucky for you if you live in the Northshore area, because you can rent a "tapmobile" to come right to your home or event. Here's what they say: "You have a choice, as two of our tapmobiles are retrofitted with 8 taps, while the pickup truck has 3 taps and Wallace has 4 Taps. Pick from a variety of our award-winning beers, and old-fashioned soda pops."

Iron Duke Brewing
100 State Street
Stockhouse 122
Ludlow, MA 01056
(413) 624-6258
www.irondukebrewing.com

Located along the Chicopee River in the historic Ludlow Mills complex, where jute was once stored, Iron Duke opened on Thanksgiving Eve 2014. After years of tinkering with a homemade nano-brewing system, and garnering awards along the learning curve, Nick Morin, his friend Michael Marcoux, and Nick's father-in-law Ron Remillard built out the 3,000-square-foot space and proceeded to run the brewery.

The guys have been busy as bees with events at the brewery, including a paint-and-sip evening to raise funds for the local youth football association's new uniforms and their second annual Sausage Fest. Here's the menu: freshly smoked kielbasa and braised cabbage with Baby-Maker mustard, Dead Nut(s) braised Italian sausage with onions and peppers, and Andouille sausage and chicken jambalaya with rice. Missed that one? Check out their Facebook page for the next fun happening. Food trucks also make an appearance regularly.

Iron Duke's beers include Baby-Maker, an Irish porter; Stockhouse 122, a hoppy pale ale; The Common, a Kentucky common ale; Dead Nuts, an American IPA; and Sinker, a "breakfast stout."

Jack's Abby
100 Clinton Street
Framingham, MA 01702
(508) 872-0900
www.jacksabbybrewing.com

All lagers, all the time, courtesy of brothers Jack, Eric, and Sam Hendler. I visited Jack's Abby on a hot day in June when they were in the old location, now happily occupied by Exhibit 'A' Brewing. We tried a few of the beers, and I especially like the Hoponius Union. We took some home, and I really enjoyed it later on a cold Saturday, when some Colby

College pals and I tailgated at a football game. Would that my alma mater's gridiron team have as much good luck and drafted talent as the brewery at Jack's!

The new place? It's huge, with long tavern tables and windows looking out to the brewery, and it's getting a lot of great reviews. Try the seared salmon entrée with a cold brew, or a wood-fired pizza, or the mussels, or . . . Well, check it out for yourselves. Oh, and there's no abbey—the name is a play on the name of Jack's wife, Abby.

John Harvard's Brew House–Framingham

1 Worcester Road
Framingham, MA 01701-5359
(508) 875-2337
www.johnharvards.com

The day we did a three-brewery tour of the Framingham area, we ducked into this location at the mall. We then wished we'd eaten lunch here instead of the place we ate that was so noisy, even at lunch, that we gave up trying to converse. Inside it has the look and feel of a quintessential British pub and tavern. Dark wood, great bar, and a hushed tone invite you to sit for a while. The brewery is behind the bar, separated by glass, so no need for a tour. Sit at the bar, watch some World Cup soccer (well, that's what we were hoping to do that day), and see the beer being made right before your eyes.

Each John Harvard's location brews its own beer, over 60 types, from light pale ales to deep, rich stouts. Brewers are given the freedom to create their own beers, rotating all the time.

John Harvard's Brew House–Harvard Square

33 Dunster Street
Cambridge, MA 02138-5002
(617) 868-3585
www.johnharvards.com

I have such fond memories of the day, *waaay* back, when I stopped here for lunch after a long morning of walking all over Boston and Cambridge to visit breweries. I literally walked from Boston to Harvard Square, and my feet were punished for weeks afterward! First of all, this location is in the old Spaghetti Emporium, a wonderful restaurant I visited as often as I could when I was a broke college student. The stained glass windows against the back wall, featuring Boston celebs like Bobby Orr, the great Bruins number four, were still there. An article in *The Harvard Crimson* in September 1973, titled "The Glutton's Guide to Harvard Square," said the place was a good option for college students to eat, with a tab for two coming to about $8, with a carafe of house wine. Yes, that was $8 for two, which is why my boyfriend and I fled there as soon as we got our work-study paychecks.

"Honest food, real beer" is not only the slogan for John Harvard's Brew House, it's the company's mission statement. Voted "Best Brewpub" two years in a row by *Boston Magazine* in the annual "Best of Boston" poll, John Harvard's continues to remain a favorite of pub-goers looking for a place where, in the words of the magazine's editors, "the beers both complement and counterpoint the American country-fare cuisine, to the satisfaction of discriminating drinkers and diners."

The dining room has been newly updated, but those stained glass windows remain. Thank goodness. Oh, and you can still order pasta, but it's worlds away from what we ate back in our college days: Bucatini with Shrimp & Bacon, "bucatini, fresh tomato sauce, shrimp, crispy bacon, basil, olive oil. $15.99."

KBC Brewery and Beer Garden at Kretschmann Brewing Company

9 Frederick Street
Webster, MA 01570-1507
(508) 671-7711
www.kbcbrewing.com

Celebrating four years in 2016, KBC is dedicated to brewing German-style ales and lagers like their Lake Lager, a Bohemian pilsner, light with a spicy hop finish. Shortly after they opened their doors in 2012, they sold out of the first 100 gallons of beer, and they were on their way.

With a newly expanded brewery and location, KBC has lots more room to brew. They have a taproom, and they have a "bring your own food" policy, so they can focus on making beer. Check the website and Facebook page for updates, like when they'll open the outdoor beer garden, who's playing what music, and their latest rotation of beers.

Lamplighter Brewing Company

284 Broadway
Cambridge, MA 02139
www.lamplighterbrewing.com

Location, location, location! The owners of Lamplighter (named after the many antique and period gas lamps that make Cambridge so charming), after a year of scouring Cambridge for a place to set up a brewery, found a former auto shop in an attractive brick building built in 1912. Cayla Marvil and A. C. Jones are doing due diligence to tear down, truck out, build up, and move in. They urge beer lovers to keep up with their blog and Facebook page for progress. Cayla writes thoughtful pieces about what I know can be an experience that can give you permanent white knuckles. Check out the blog at www.lamplighterbrewing.com/blog to follow the progress. Looking good!

Lefty's Brewing Company

301 Wells Street
Greenfield, MA 01337-0124
(413) 475-3449
www.leftysbrew.com

Bill "Lefty" Goldfarb and his wife Melissa own this brewery, which opened in 2010. Since that time, they've produced over 25 beers, all made lovingly and with mostly local ingredients. Their team has now expanded to include seven more dedicated members.

Since a lot of beer drinkers are on the hop wagon, here is their brewer's description of the IPA (6.6% ABV), a year-round member of the menu: "Lefty's English style IPA is brewed up with whole leaf Chinook and Cascade hops . . . [It] releases strong hints of citrus flavors with a crisp bite, yet is well balanced."

All of their beer descriptions suggest ideal food pairings, something that should help you out if you have any doubts! Lefty's also partners with local eateries to put on beer dinners, and they rent out their space for special events.

Mayflower Brewing Company
12 Resnik Road, Suite 3
Plymouth, MA 02360-7245
(508) 746-2674
www.mayflowerbrewing.com

There's a factoid that goes something like this: If everyone who claimed to have an ancestor who came over on the *Mayflower* really did, there would have been hundreds of people on board. Or maybe it was thousands. Who's your *Mayflower* ancestor? Mine was DeGory Priest, who left London "under a cloud," according to some family lore. (Probably a cloud of evaporated beer.)

Here's Mayflower's story, in their words: "Mayflower Brewing Company is a craft beer microbrewery located in historic Plymouth, Massachusetts. Founded in 2007 by a tenth great grandson of John Alden, beer barrel cooper on board the *Mayflower*, we are dedicated to celebrating the history and legacy of the Pilgrims by creating unique, high-quality ales for the New England market."

This very professional and homey brewery has what a lot of them have, but seems to do things just right: the retail store, tasting room, and, of course, the beers, which are available in most New England states. Since this style is one of my favorites, I give you the brewer's description of their Porter (5.2% ABV), available year-round: "Mayflower Porter is a rich, complex brew that is smooth and full-flavored. Five varieties of malted barley provide notes of roasted coffee beans and bittersweet chocolate with a hint of smokiness."

Medusa Brewing Company

111 Main Street
Hudson, MA 01749-2210
(978) 310-1933
www.medusabrewing.com

Stop the presses! When I checked in with Medusa, it had just announced it had won at the Craft Brewers Conference. The beer was their Ducho-vni, a Czech pils. Handshakes all around, guys!

I was excited when I learned that a craft brewery was going into the town of Hudson. I grew up in nearby Littleton, and like many mill towns in New England, Hudson was and is experiencing a renaissance with beer and food. Keith Antul and an ample crew are doing the brewing, Keith "Sully" Sullivan is the general manager and co-owner, and co-owner Tom Sutter presides over the ledgers and brews a few. The taproom contains a 50-foot-long bar and handmade mahogany tables. Add to that a vital "scene" where Medusa offers open mic and trivia nights and yoga. Wait, what? Yup. Yoga some mornings.

Two hoppy beers recently available in their taproom were Futurist (6.5% ABV), an India pale lager with "intense, lush citrus and tropical fruit character from a luxurious combination of Galaxy, Citra, and Azacca hops, fermented with our German lager yeast"; and Albatross #5 (6.8% ABV), an American IPA that is "hopped entirely with southern hemi-sphere varieties: This round features Topaz from Australia, and Wakatu and Rakau from New Zealand."

Merrimack Ales

92 Bolt Street
Lowell, MA 01852
(978) 799-9480
www.merrimackales.com

Since opening in 2015, Merrimack's Adam Pearson and crew have been delighting Lowell with beers like Alt Hypothesis, their take on an Altbier, and First Article, a dry-hopped rye IPA. They were also trying to sweet-talk moms everywhere with a Facebook post in May 2016 announcing Honey White Ale and Chocolate Stout available for sale in the brewery.

Merrimack is a neighbor to Navigation Brewing Company, so you can get double the fun with a visit, then a dose of history at the Lowell mill museum.

Mystic Brewery
174 Williams Street
Chelsea, MA 02150-3804
(617) 800-9023
www.mystic-brewery.com

Mystic gets high marks from visitors for friendly staff and great beers, both essential criteria for a successful brewery and tasting room. Their mission "to make distinctly regional, naturally beautiful beers using artisanal methods and indigenous yeast cultures" got them short-listed in an article on Craving Boston (http://cravingboston.wgbh.org), part of the great WGBH family of websites devoted to food and drink. Mystic's owner, Louie Berceli, talked about his beers in "Here's Why You Should Hop on the Sour Beer Bandwagon" by Luke O'Neil, explaining what sour beers are, and what they are not, but essentially saying, "It's just a beer that's sour." Oh, and so much more, which he explains. For example, there are those wild yeasts involved, including the elusive Brettanomyces, that give the beers a particular flavor.

Mystic's website is up to date with what's available on tap and in bottles. A recent release called Letters After Z was described as a dry-hopped sour ale with 3.6% ABV and another was Frequency of the Sky, a kettle-soured saison dry-hopped with Wakatu hops.

Nashoba Valley Winery and Brewery / Bolton Beer Works
100 Wattaquadock Hill Road
Bolton, MA 01740-1238
(978) 779-5521
www.nashobawinery.com

When I found out that Nashoba Valley was brewing beer, I was so happy. It gave me an excuse to go back for a visit, which I did on Mother's Day, passing through to Maine after visiting my son. This is a destination because of the beautiful grounds and orchards, even if it's for a short visit to pick up some beer, or wine, or spirits. They make all three. In fact, way back in 1983 I lived down the road from them and got a job there as a salesperson. Didn't last long, as I had two very little kids back then, a babysitter that lived a half-hour away (in the wrong direction), and people in the booze biz didn't want to sample wine in the mid-morning. Considering that the beer bus tours I've been on start at 10:30 a.m., I think those folks just didn't know how to have fun.

Brewer Jeffrey Matthew makes a nice selection of beers, some available in bottles and some as growler fills. Try the Heron Ale, Double Rye IPA, and Blueberry Ale, among others. Call ahead to see what's on tap.

New City Brewery
180 Pleasant Street
Easthampton, MA 01027
(413) 529-2000
www.newcitybrewery.com

Who is your favorite character on *Gilligan's Island*? If you said Ginger, you'd be right on the money, as this ingredient (not Ginger the person) is the focus of brewer Sam Dibble's flagship beer. In their words: "Bursting with the aroma of fresh ginger, with an effervescent bite and a clean, crisp finish, New City Ginger Beer has subtle notes of tropical pineapple and citrus that complement its distinctive zip of ginger, with a slight hint of molasses."

If ginger is not your favorite palate-pleaser, fear not: New City brews over a dozen types of beer. Besides the flagship ginger, they have Connecticut River Kolsch, Signature IPA, Dauntless Dry Stout, and Minuteman Pale Ale as their mainstays. Their tasting room, which includes a reclaimed bar from Fenway Park, bursts with old mill charm. And with their weekly Brewmaster's Jazz events, the music and the beer are rocking Easthampton!

Newburyport Brewing Company
4 New Pasture Road
Newburyport, MA 01950-4040
(978) 463-8700
www.nbptbrewing.com

Brewmaster Mike Robinson has almost two decades of home and professional brewing experience, and he's the one who makes Newburyport's beers. Among them: Newburyport Pale Ale, which is now available on the Delta Northeast Shuttle; Plum Island Belgian White; and Greenhead IPA. Owners Chris Webb and Bill Fisher are musicians as well as the kind of guys who think every adventure should be accompanied with a good beer in hand, and they offer their stage at the brewery for local musicians to play. In fact, every Thursday, Friday, and Saturday evening from 5 to 8 p.m., there's live music at the brewery. The beers are available in Massachusetts, Rhode Island, and southern New Hampshire, but they are growing fast and may be headed your way.

Night Shift Brewing
87 Santilli Highway
Everett, MA 02149-2405
(617) 294-4233
www.nightshiftbrewing.com

Founders Michael Oxton, Mike O'Mara, and Rob Burns began brewing in their apartment in Somerville. Because they all had day jobs, they brewed at night, hence the name Night Shift. In a great video on their website, they look like mad millennial scientists, stirring and sniffing their way through batch after batch. After years of developing their palates, their recipes, and their plan, they opened the brewery in 2012. Their hard work has paid off: In May 2016 they took the bronze in the IPA category at the World Beer Cup. Here's the brewer's description for the winning Santilli: "Smooth-sipping, with massive hop profile. It is crisp, tropical and delicious; named after our address on Santilli Highway in Everett. 6% ABV."

Night Shift was featured in a Craving Boston article by Luke O'Neil titled "Here's Why You Should Hop on the Sour Beer Bandwagon" (http://cravingboston.wgbh.org). And here's why you should visit if you like that tang: Duchess, "a 5.1% saison fermented with sauvignon blanc grape must, this effervescent farmhouse ale has a crisp, vinous character."

No food is served, but you are invited to bring your own. They also have visiting food trucks.

Northampton Brewery

11 Brewster Court
Northampton, MA 01060-3801
(413) 584-9903
www.northamptonbrewery.com

Part of their interesting story, in their words: "In 1986 after a chance visit to the Front Street Brewpub in Santa Cruz, California, sister and brother, Janet and Peter Egelston became excited at the prospect of putting all other goals on hold to pursue a dream of becoming brewpub owners."

Northampton opened in 1987 and as such was the second brewpub to open in Massachusetts, the first being Commonwealth Brewing Company. CBC is no longer with us, leaving Janet Egleston's brewpub with the distinction of being the oldest in the Bay State. It is consistently voted Pioneer Valley's best brewpub by the Valley Advocate Readers' Poll. Sister companies are Smuttynose and Portsmouth Brewery in New Hampshire.

A delectable-sounding beer from their varied menu is Blue Boots IPA (6% ABV), with the brewer's description: "Huge pine aroma, intense resinous hop flavor, and an extremely dry finish leave you with a magnificently unbalanced IPA. Not bound by geography, Blue Boots is neither a 'West Coast' nor 'East Coast' IPA."

Notch Brewing

23 Hayward Street
Ipswich, MA 01938-2044
(978) 853-9138
www.notchbrewing.com

Notch was the first brewery to make session ales only, the types of beers you can drink a few of over the course of a family barbecue or beach day you don't want to end, without having to get a cab afterward. (No guarantees there, but you get the idea.) My friend Nate Byrnes wrote a great blog post about sessionable ales that you can read at www.goodbrew hunting.com. Here's what he has to say about their IPA:

> *Fortunately for us, Massachusetts is the home of an excellent session-only brewery: Notch Brewing, whose owner and brewer Chris Lohring makes no beer bigger than 4.5%. I haven't had a bad brew by them, and their Left of the Dial IPA (4.3%) may very well be the best session IPA out there. Mildly grapefruity, slightly floral, lightly bready, and entirely yummy, this is a session beer worth seeking out.*

Chris Lohring, the session ale king and "independent brewer" who has brewed since the early days of the beer boom, makes the beers at Ipswich, Two Roads, and Kennebunkport brewing companies. Notch has no brewery of their own. Find the beers using the beer finder tool on their website, and watch Facebook and Twitter for news of events where they'll appear to pour the beer. Available throughout Massachusetts and southern Maine.

Offshore Ale Company

30 Kennebec Avenue
Oak Bluffs, MA 02557
(508) 693-2626
www.offshoreale.com

Open since 1997, Offshore Ale is *the* island destination if you are going to "Martha's." Neal Atkins brews up a couple dozen beers that rotate with the seasons and complement the largely pub-style menu that also features wood-fired pizza and grown-up entrees of seafood, pasta, Portuguese fisherman's stew, and burgers. Of course, you can also get oysters on the half shell or a lobster roll! Or try this, say with an award-winning East Chop Lighthouse Ale: the Brewhouse Pulled Pork Sandwich, made with pork slow-cooked overnight in a blend of their homemade root beer and Nut Brown Ale, then mixed with a honey BBQ sauce.

Opa Opa Brewing Company
4 Main Street
Williamsburg, MA 01096
(413) 527-8282
www.opaopabrewing.com

The beers—among them Opa Opa Light, Honesty 47 Pale Ale, and Buckwheat IPA—are available in parts of Massachusetts and Connecticut. They began with a 10 bbl system at the restaurant in Southampton in 2004 and now produce the bulk of the beer at the brewery. Some of the beers are served only at the brewpub, so it's fun to know you're getting a brew you can't get elsewhere. You can also try them at the Opa Opa Steakhouse at 169 College Highway in Southampton. This is a cowboy-themed steakhouse with all the usual food suspects. They have a huge menu, featuring steaks, chicken, seafood, lots of appetizers, salads, and soups. I hear the gorgonzola steak is amazing.

Paper City Brewery Company
108 Cabot Street
Holyoke, MA 01040-6061
(413) 535-1588
www.papercity.com

Paper City is the culmination of a home brewer's dream, as all of them are, right? Opening in 1995 with their flagship Holyoke Dam Ale, Paper City is the love child of Jay Hebert. With a newer head brewer, Ben Anhalt (the first was Ben Quackenbush), the brewery now puts out several styles and contract brews for other craft breweries. Since a character in my novel-in-progress is named Riley, and he's a bartender, I'll give you the brewer's description of their stout: "Riley's Stout is an Irish style with a rich chocolate color and frothy tan head."

On November 14, 2014, Hunter Styles wrote in his *Valley Advocate* column "The Beerhunter:" "Paper City opened in 1995, and they've been hosting open house nights since 1998. They're not the new kids on the block anymore. But no other spot in the Valley offers such a cheap way to enjoy free-flowing beer and live entertainment—local bands rotate through on Friday nights—in such a funky, unusual setting."

My Holyoke experience pales in comparison to these open house parties. I attended Immaculate Conception school in the mid-sixties. Biggest event of the week was running up the street on Fridays to buy greasy and delicious fish-and-chips for 50 cents and bringing it back to the cafeteria for lunch. Yum. But no beer.

The People's Pint / Franklin County Brewing Co.
76 Hope Street
Greenfield, MA 01301-3573
(413) 773-0333
www.thepeoplespint.com

Live from Hophead (www.beer-journal.com), intrepid traveler and sampler of all things beer and food:

Living in Massachusetts affords me the opportunity to enjoy a wide variety of fine breweries, pubs, restaurants, and farms; the People's Pint in downtown Greenfield perfectly blends the best characteristics from each of these into a paradise for beer geeks, foodies, locavores, and friends of planet Earth. The passionate and welcoming folks at the Pint pour their own expertly crafted beers, bake incredible desserts, create exquisite dishes from scratch based on seasonal New England fruits and vegetables, and, whenever possible, use organic foods supplied by local farmers and producers. As if this were not enough to make you fall in love with them, they use no disposable plastics or paper napkins, all food scraps are composted, all plastic, cardboard, paper, glass and metal is recycled, and the spent brewery grain is fed to local pigs and goats. As a result of these sustainable practices, the Pint has never disposed of more than one barrel of trash each day since opening their doors in 1997.

What is a visit to the People's Pint like, you ask? The most wonderful aromas greet you as you walk through the door to the cozy and intimate brewpub. Did I mention that they also smoke their own meats? Seating is available at the bar, in booths, or at tables in the dining area, and at a high counter facing the windows and Federal Street beyond. The food menus and specials are creative and varied with plenty of options to suit any taste, including vegetarians and those with food allergies and/or sensitivities.

I saved the best for last: the beer! Much like the food, the ingredients used during the brewing process are always fresh and sourced locally when available. The Pint keeps it interesting with a combination of year-round, seasonal, collaborative, one-off, and cask-conditioned beers. If you are a beer lover and find yourself anywhere near Greenfield, a stop at the People's Pint is a must.

Percival Beer Company
Dorchester, MA 02122
(781) 664-4705
www.percivalbeercompany.com

His own brewery, the dream of Felipe Oliviera, who grew up on Percival Street in Dorchester, isn't quite a reality yet. When I checked in with Felipe, he told me that they were "working with the city to find the right place." And it most certainly will have a tasting room. Meantime, their beers, Dot Ale 1630 and Hip Hop IPA, are being made by Mercury Brewing in Ipswich. In 2016, Percival added four more beer styles to their family.

Dorchester is being transformed from a time-worn neighborhood to a vibrant, diverse place that has embraced Percival's beers. Stay tuned to see where they locate the brewery, which Felipe says will "have a community atmosphere and be a cultural center where we'll educate the public about the history of Dorchester." Check out their website for retail establishments that sell and serve their beers in and around Boston. And don't miss the hilarious television commercial, which aired during Red Sox games, on the website.

Portico Brewing Company

Cambridge, MA 02138
(617) 694-5198
www.porticobrewing.com

Owners and brewers Alex Zielke and Alex Rabe opened Portico in 2012 and "gypsy brew" the beers, originally at Watch City in Waltham and now at Mercury Brewing in Ipswich. The "gypsy'" part means the guys make their own beer, but without the overhead of owning their own facility. Think Pretty Things Beer & Ale Project when it was around.

In 2016 Portico announced their new Escher series, named for the Dutch graphic designer M. C. Escher. Each release of this American pale ale style will feature a unique hop blend. Use the "find it" toggle on the website to find their beers, including the flagship Fuzzy Logic, their take on a traditional Kölsch, and Chroma, an amber ale brewed with rye.

Rapscallion Brewery & Tap Room

195 Arnold Road
Fiskdale, MA 01518
(508) 347-7500
www.drinkrapscallion.com

Located in a former cider barn on the 150-acre Hyland family orchard, this is where Rapscallion started out. You can still visit and sample the beers and even do some yoga, followed by beer, of course. In April 2016 they announced their new beer, Glacier IPA, a single-malt, single-hop beer made with Glacier hops and pale malt. The taproom is always jumping with trivia, live music, and sometimes disc golf (outside, of course). Check their Facebook page for special events and news, such as the new wrinkle of food trucks coming to the brewery the first Friday of the month. And once a year, they sponsor the Hop Head Fest.

Rapscallion Table & Tap

5 Strawberry Hill Road
Acton, MA 01720
(978) 429-8161
www.drinkrapscallion.com

I could go on forever about the building where Rapscallion opened its second location. Acton is the next town over from Littleton, where I grew up. I worked in Acton, a sleepy suburb of Boston, which we then dubbed "Action, Mass" because, of course, we thought it was without "action" at all. The old home Rapscallion was so lucky to get used to house a beloved and sorely missed genuine-article French restaurant called Chez Claude. I had my very first, and I think only, chateaubriand for two there. This small-looking house is really sprawling inside and dates from the 1700s. It appears that every single detail, including the old fireplaces and colonial architecture, has been preserved. In fact, when I visited, I was entranced by the history of the place. I half expected the owner to be wearing a tri-cornered hat. Okay, enough with the history geek rambling.

Twin brothers Cedric and Peter Daniel own both the Acton Table & Tap and the Fiskdale brewery and taproom where they started. Peter married Chez Claude owner Claude Miquel's daughter, and although Claude ceased operating his restaurant, he had held onto the property. No-brainer to put another Rapscallion there. They change up the food menu enough to keep people coming back, and they tempt by showing pictures of some of the dishes on their Facebook page. One new dish announced when I checked in, Kumquat-Glazed Salmon, was described as "Faroe Island salmon, toasted couscous cakes and Asian purple cabbage slaw." Their flagship beer, Honey, an extra pale ale made with local wildflower honey, would go quite nicely with that salmon.

Rock Bottom Brewery–Stuart Street

115 Stuart Street
Boston, MA 02116-5609
(617) 742-2739
www.rockbottom.com

Begun in 1991 in Denver, Colorado, Rock Bottom was a brewery/restaurant and the collaboration of a brewer and an entrepreneur. Twenty-five years and many locations and awards later, they are going strong. The beers are brewed at their location in Pittsburgh and shipped to Boston, I was told by the nice man who answered the phone. They are vehement that the beers are fresh and expertly made. There is a list of about a half dozen that would appeal to just about anyone, and each location's brewmaster has free rein to create a beer he or she wants to make. That means ask for the Brewmaster's Choice if you want the most local brew you can find here.

The food menu is huge and offers many pub items such as burgers, but also interesting entrees and appetizers. They list a chef and a sous chef, but it would be better if they included the names of the brewers, just so people can feel like they are truly drinking house-made beer.

Slesar Bros. Brewing Co. / Beer Works
www.beerworks.net

Boston Beer Works
61 Brookline Avenue
Boston, MA 02215-3406
(617) 536-2337

Boston Beer Works
112 Canal Street
Boston, MA 02114-1805
(617) 896-2337

Framingham Beer Works
345 Cochituate Road
Framingham, MA 01701-4607
(508) 309-3373

Hingham Beer Works
18 Shipyard Drive
Hingham, MA 02043-1670
(781) 749-2337

Lowell Beer Works
203 Cabot Street
Lowell, MA 01854-3620
(978) 937-2337

Salem Beer Works
278 Derby Street
Salem, MA 01970-3635
(978) 745-2337

Slesar Bros. was created when brothers Joe and Steve Slesar desired better beer. Sound familiar? They opened Boston Beer Works in 1992 and haven't looked back since. Now boasting six locations, Beer Works offers over 50 variations of lagers, ales, stouts, and pilsners each year and keeps 15 craft beers on tap at each location at any given time. Each location has its own brewery, and they have a production brewery. The menu is a big one, with this delicious-sounding rendition of mac and cheese: Shrimp 'n Ham 'n Mac 'n Cheese, "shrimp, Canadian bacon and spinach with cavatappi in a rich, golden cheese sauce infused with our own oatmeal stout and topped with buttery crumbs."

Somerville Brewing Company / Slumbrew

American Fresh Brewhouse Brewery + Taproom
15 Ward Street
Somerville, MA 02143
(800) 428-1150
www.slumbrew.com/Boynton_Brewery

Growing in leaps and bounds from their tiny test-lab brewery of old, Caitlin Jewell and Jeff Leiter have kept growing and adding venues in which to enjoy their hit beers since their beginning in 2011. At the Ward Street address is the brewery and taproom, where you can sit and dine from a wide menu of everything from charcuterie platters to sandwiches, salads, and starters. Flatbreads, anyone? And then there are the beers. The newest ones were Niles Crane Blonde Ale, Scooter Strawberry Wheat, and a gluten-removed option called {GF} Yourself. But don't stop there. Limited-batch releases as well as old favorites abound. Go for the Liquid Courage Comedy Club night or Taphouse Trivia.

American Fresh Brewhouse Beer Garden
310 Canal Street
Somerville, MA 02145
(800) 428-1150
www.slumbrew.com/Assembly_Row

This is a funky, fun, family-friendly beer garden with a menu that complements the beers. Open year-round and tented and heated in winter, the beer garden is located at Assembly Row, near Legoland, retail shopping, and the Assembly Row T stop. Live bands play on Saturday nights, and on Sunday there's trivia. There's even a kids' menu with a deconstructed Fluffernutter and mac and cheese. Check the website for which beers appear on tap: Trippel Trekker, Flagraiser DIPA, Old Sol Bloodorange Hefeweizen, Gose Revolution, and Island Day Pale Ale have all shared billing. Any of these would wet my whistle with their Signature Charcuterie Plate: Imperial Spicy Chorizo Calabrese Salami, Alps Sopresatta, Cabot Aged Vermont Cheddar, Great Hill Blue Cheese, Doves and Figs Jam, Fresh Fruit, Taza Chocolate, and Mango Cashews by Q's Nuts Crostini.

Spencer Brewery
167 North Spencer Road
Spencer, MA 01562-1232
www.spencerbrewery.com

Sorry, but you are most likely not going to get a tour of this brewery, since that would violate the rules of the monastery. But these monks are hard at work, and there are many events you can attend. Watch the Facebook page. The beer is available even here in Maine!

I am familiar with Spencer Abbey because my father's family is from Spencer. The monks have been supporting themselves for decades by making and selling jams and jellies under the label Trappist Preserves. When one of the monks got brewing "fever," they began exploring brewing as a way to become more self-supporting, which is one of the tenets of the Benedictine Order. After a two-year data-gathering effort, which involved traveling all over Belgium talking to brewers and drinking great beer, the dream became reality. They even had a special glass designed to hold the only Trappist ale licensed in the United States.

In their words:

Our recipe was inspired by the traditional refectory ales known as patersbier ("fathers' beer" in Flemish) in Belgium. These sessionable beers are brewed by the monks for their dinner table and are typically only available at the monastery. Spencer is a full-bodied, golden-hued ale with fruity accents, a dry finish and light hop bitterness. The beer is unfiltered and unpasteurized, preserving live yeast that naturally carbonates the beer in the bottle and keg and contributes to the beer flavor and aroma.

The Tap Brewing Company
100 Washington Street
Haverhill, MA 01832-5500
(978) 374-1117
www.tapbrewingcompany.com

Love the tagline: You eat and drink. We brew and cook. Let's hang out.

Located in a historic 1882 building that once housed a leather company and a millworkers' bar, the Tap has been brewing in Haverhill since 2003. Most of the brewing can be seen right from the dining area, so tours are of the armchair variety. The 10 bbl brewing system produces enough beer to keep eight to nine brews on tap at all times. They also package and distribute to stores and restaurants throughout Massachusetts.

Tempting the palate around Christmas was this special: grilled swordfish topped with Argentinean chimichurri, served with mashed and roasted asparagus. A recommended pairing was the Bitter Rival (7.3% ABV), described as follows: "Brewed like a west coast style IPA with a heinous amount of Columbus, Amarillo and Chinook. A heavy-handed focus on bitterness is what this one is all about. We named this brew in honor of our boundless disdain for a particular hockey club in Montreal. Hops and hockey are both better when they're bitter. It's science."

The menu is on the small side but has plenty of variety, even offering a few vegetarian options. Head to the hometown of John Greenleaf Whittier or you will regret it. After all, in the poet's words, "For all sad words of tongue and pen, the saddest are these, 'It might have been.'" Do it. Go.

Tree House Brewery
160 East Hill Road
Monson, MA 01057-9203
(413) 523-2367
www.treehousebrew.com

"Sorry folks, we have completely run out of beer," said Tree House's Facebook post before Christmas 2014. This little brewery-that-could has taken New England by storm. Lines out the door of people waiting for growler fills at this draft-only brewery validate *BeerAdvocate*'s assessment of Tree House's Julius American IPA as 55th in its listing of 250 best beers in the world. Ponder that one.

After expanding in 2015, from 1 employee and 55 barrels of cellar space to 13 employees and 650 barrels of cellar space, cofounder Nate Lanier announced another expansion, this one combined with a move to nearby Charlton, Massachusetts. Projected to be completed in 2017, the massive facility is, said Nate on the website blog, "designed as an expandable and multi-faceted 45,000 square foot facility and will feature a state of the art 50 BBL brewhouse, a 5,000 square foot retail space where can sales, bottle sales, and full pours will be offered at least five days a week, and a large outdoor pavilion." This means more beers, more availability, and a gathering place to enjoy it all. The Monson operation will continue until 2017, when the new place is up and running. As ever, watch the website and Facebook for updates.

Here's the brewer's description of their heralded Julius IPA: "Bursting with 1.6 oz per gallon of American hops, Julius is loaded with notes of passionfruit, mango, and citrus. At 6.5% alcohol, it is refreshing and freakishly drinkable."

Trillium Brewing–Boston, Fort Point
369 Congress Street
Boston, MA 02210-1836
(617) 453-8745
www.trilliumbrewing.com

J. C. and Esther Tetreault are the husband-and-wife team who dared to open a brewery within the city limits of Boston, and it's taken off like the shot heard round the world. Open for growler fills and bottle sales, the Fort Point Trillium has at least seven beers on hand at a time. They do impose bottle limits on some of the brews.

When I spoke with a brewery staff member, he told me they'd just released Stonington, named after the town in Connecticut where the wild yeast originates. J. C. and Esther were married at Stonington Vineyards, and they take the yeast from the skins of the grapes there and use them for this beer. Rated as "outstanding" on *BeerAdvocate*, Stonington may or may not be available again. But that's the fun of visiting these local breweries. You never know what surprise awaits! Like that 10 bbl batch of Idaho 7, available only in growlers. Storm the gates, people.

Trillium Brewing Company–Canton
110 Shawmut Road
Canton, MA 02021
(781) 562-0073
www.trilliumbrewing.com

Opened in 2015, Trillium's Canton location offers a little bit more than the Fort Point brewery: You can have 2-ounce samples in addition to growler fills and bottle sales. No food is offered, but that's the case at a lot of places. Grab your growler and get yourself to one of the fine local eateries. No fewer than five DIPAs were available when this book went to press, along with other beers including an Imperial stout made with cold-brewed coffee called Night and Day a new pale ale called Idaho 7, first in their Permutations series, described as "a 4.5% ABV with aromas & flavors of lemon pith, apricot, white grape, rustic grain."

Wachusett Brewing Company
175 State Road East
Westminster, MA 01473-1208
(978) 874-9965
www.wachusettbrew.com

That was then: The president and co-owner of Wachusett, twenty-six-year-old Ned LaFortune III, has a clear vision of what his company is and where it's going. He and his partners, head brewer Peter Quinn and plan engineer Kevin Buckler, were classmates at nearby Worcester Polytechnic Institute, all studying for careers in various technical fields. While working as a project engineer for an architect firm, LaFortune began home-brewing and planning his own brewery. When they were ready to take the plunge, the three partners quit their jobs, hit up friends and family for capital, and launched Wachusett Brewing Company. Less than four months after their opening, the trio had to quadruple their output to keep up with customer demand, and they are already being approached by Boston-area restaurants and bars that want to carry their ales. LaFortune, however, insists that WBC has no intention of expanding beyond Massachusetts. The beer: Country Ale, WBC's flagship beer, is smooth, full-bodied and dark brown in color, with a rich, malty finish.

This is now: Well, that resolution was broken! Celebrating 20 years in 2014, WBC is now distributed all over New England and in New York and New Jersey. Their year-round beer offerings are Country Pale Ale, IPA, Blueberry Ale, Green Monsta IPA, Nut Brown Ale, Black Shack Porter, Light IPA, Larry Imperial IPA, and Strawberry White. Check their website and Facebook page for new releases and seasonals. If you go out for a tour, you can have lunch at Gardner Ale House, a brewpub in nearby Gardner. It's worth the 15 minutes to get there, and you can get a taste of Rich Walton's beers while you're at it.

Wandering Star Brewing Company

11 Gifford Street
Pittsfield, MA 01201-3701
(347) 524-5845 or (413) 717-7041
www.wanderingstarbrewing.com

Open since 2011, this is a production brewery that doesn't offer a bar or food, but they do give tours and growler fills. Chris Post and his wife, Shannon, head up the team at Wandering Star, which also includes Chris Cuzme (the two Chrises are alumni of the New York City Homebrewers Guild) and Alex Hall, a former *Ale Street News* columnist and alum of England's Dark Star Brewery. Shannon and Chris moved up to Massachusetts from New York to open the brewery. In a post-Christmas phone call, Shannon told me, "I still commute a few days a week to New York to work a day job, but I help out when I can."

Their year-round beers include Mild at Heart (4.4% ABV), described as "a 'Dark Mild' English style session beer with the ABV and color of an Irish Stout but a nuttier, softer mouthfeel from crystal and chocolate malts, and a finishing dryness from aroma hops. Conceived for cask and perfect served as a Real Ale." In June 2016 Wandering Star celebrated its fifth anniversary with a party at the brewery. Watch their Facebook page for special events and new beers.

Westfield River Brewing Company

707 College Highway
Southwick, MA 01077
(413) 374-8425
www.westfieldriverbrewing.com

Westfield River is a destination taproom brewery, focusing on high-quality, small-batch beers. They offer 10 rotating taps and in March 2016 announced that Granddaddy Frank's BBQ will be located right in the brewery. "Died and gone to heaven" is all I have to say. The barbecue joint will have the same hours as the brewery, so no fears of getting shut out of that burrito. Gaylon Stanley, owner and chef, lived in San Antonio, Texas, for 20 years and is creating a menu with simple and fresh Cajun, Tex-Mex, soul, and comfort food influences.

Okay, now for the beer: Among the several on tap are Americana (5.6% ABV), a hoppy ale with Citra and Amarillo hops; Bad Boy (8.2% ABV), an imperial IPA brewed with Motueka hops; and Session IPA (4.5% ABV), with a light body and tropical fruit hops. The brewery events just don't stop: live music, beer dinners, and a spring fest, just to name a few.

Wormtown Brewing

72 Shrewsbury Street, Unit 4
Worcester, MA 01604
(774) 239-1555
www.wormtownbrewery.com

I tracked down brewer/owner Ben Roesch when he was planning the move to this bigger facility. I asked him his brewing background. "My first professional job was at Cambridge Brewing Company from fall of 2001 to about the fall of 2002," he replied. "I worked at Wachusett at the same time, then became full-time brewer at Wachusett until spring of 2004. I became head brewer and distiller at Nashoba Valley until 2007." Ben also did some consulting/brewing for Bentley brewing.

That new place opened in January 2015. Hop ahead to 2016, when Ben announced that Spencer Brewery, the only licensed Trappist brewery in the United States, will contract brew for them. Seems Wormtown's demand is exceeding their ability to make it, which is the formula for happy beer drinkers everywhere. Spencer will be making some of Wormtown's seasonal beers, so Ben and his crew can turn out more Be Hoppy and Hopulence, among other favorites. Not only that, but in April 2016 Wormtown earned a Best in Worcester award for best craft brewery. As for the beer, one fan said, "Be Hoppy is love in liquid form." Visit this great Worcester success story, drink the beers, and enjoy the events.

Massachusetts Beer Bus Tours

Boston Brew Tours

(617) 453-TOUR

www.bostonbrewtours.com

Chad Brodsky and his crew will bring you around to some of Boston's best breweries, beer bars, and even a meadery. Here's what their "original tour" is composed of: "The Original Brew Tour showcases a tasting of up to 18 different beers, delectable lunch and beer pairing at Meadhall, and round-trip transportation from Beacon Hill. The Original Tour gives you an exclusive look into how one of Boston's premier beer bars maintains 100 different beers on draft."

New England Brewery Tours

(617) 539-6055

www.newenglandbrewerytours.com

Matt Savage wants people to know how unique his tour package is: Included in the fee is door-to-door transportation within a 5-mile radius of downtown Boston (to help folks out from behind the wheel of a car after an afternoon of tasting brews), a four-course meal paired with four beers, tours and tastings at at least three breweries, and a professional guide who will educate tour-goers on the nuances of craft beer.

According to Matt, "We give tours to the public from Tuesdays through Saturdays and will customize private tours for birthdays or corporate events. We mostly go to Boston area breweries and brewpubs, but we'll go anywhere for a private charter. We've been to New Hampshire and up to Portland, as well as out to Framingham to Jack's Abby."

In addition to the breweries listed on the website, NEBT is adding more and more to their list. They are selective, choosing places based on the quality of their beer and service, and they structure the tours to give customers a contrast in styles and flavors.

"Tours are my full-time work," Matt said, "and it's getting busier. We opened in 2012 and people love what we do." When I asked what are the must-do breweries, he replied, "It depends on what customers want. Some people want to visit Sam Adams and Harpoon because they're well-known. Others want to see the newer breweries and smaller places. We go to both Sam Adams and Harpoon, but also travel to Idle Hands, Trillium, Jack's Abby, and Aeronaut in Somerville. There's a huge variety, and we're adding more every day."

New Hampshire

THE GRANITE STATE USED TO BE THE DRIVE-TO PLACE TO BUY BEER when the stores were closed in Massachusetts on Sunday. Ahh, those were the bad old days. Now you can head up and taste dozens of carefully crafted, delicious beers. In winter, there is skiing; in summer, beautiful beaches. The Old Man of the Mountain is no longer all there, as the distinguished profile of a wise old fellow broke off some years ago, but tiny colonial towns coexist with reemerging cities, like Manchester, where the old mill town is now burgeoning with craft beers and upscale dining. Visit the country where Robert Frost penned these words: "Two roads diverged in a yellow wood . . ." Would *you* take the road less traveled?

603 Brewery
12 Liberty Drive, Unit 7
Londonderry, NH 03053-2286
(603) 630-7745
www.603brewery.com

So many craft brewers meet their business partners in college, it makes me wonder when any studying got done. But thank goodness down time is allowed in the ivory tower, or else we'd be experiencing a beer drought instead of this brew heaven. Okay, the three people who started 603 in 2012 met in college, but they weren't running around reciting Robert Burns poems (that would be okay, too). There was some engineering and chemistry being learned, as well as marketing, and those subjects are crucial to running a successful brewery.

Growing from a nanobrewery to one using a 15-barrel system in just two years, 603 is open for tours and tastings; you can also fill your growler or buy bombers or cans. Use the beer finder on the website to track retail outlets that carry their beers, including Winni Ale, an amber ale, which according to the website is still their most popular beer; 18 Mile Rye Pale Ale; White Peaks, a white IPA; Cogway IPA; and 9th State Red IPA. Taste the beers and get their back stories from owners Dan, Geoff, and Tamsin.

I caught Geoff on a cool October afternoon. Although he is clear that he doesn't want 603 to become a brewpub, they do want to offer some food. "We've experimented with reselling pizza from Giovanni's, our local pizza joint. We serve gourmet popcorn, a real hit, which we give with a flight of samples." For travelers who want a full meal, Geoff recommends Poorboy's for breakfast and Giovanni's Roast Beef & Pizza or New England Tap House for lunch or dinner.

7th Settlement Brewery
47 Washington Street
Dover, NH 03820
(603) 373-1001
www.7thsettlement.com

I'm writing this on a cold, wet, gray day in Maine. What's new, you ask? Why should Kate think "almost-winter," a fifth season in Maine, would be different this year? But as my eyes wander over 7th Settlement's lunch menu, I have faith that I'll get through, if I can just have some of their signature dishes. How about "ten beer-brined free bird wings with choice of ginger cider glazed or damn hot," or "daily-made brewer's bread with beer-cheese fondue," or for the carnivores, a burger, specifically "the grilled heritage 1868 grind topped with batch 7 sauce, aged cheddar, smoked bacon, lettuce, tomato & onion"? Oh and give me a side of hop-salted fries. What the heck, I'll finish with chocolate bacon cake or apple ale cobbler. What calories? It's time to get ready to hibernate.

Beer? Of course! Brewers Josh Henry and Nate Sephton make Peter Peter Pumpkin Brown and Dry Irish Stout, among others including

Bully Boy whiskey-barrel-aged imperial brown, which they urge you to get before it's gone. Sound tempting? That's the beauty of "local." I may never be able to get that beer in Maine, but it sure makes me put 7th Settlement on my beer bucket list.

Anheuser-Busch Brewery

221 Daniel Webster Highway
Merrimack, NH 03054-4807
(603) 889-6631
www.budweisertours.com

If you're in a fight with big beer, maybe it's time to get over it. For a few hours. Taking a tour of a big-beer brewery can be a great contrast and alternative to the nanobrewery tour and tasting. In a blog called New Hampshire Kids, the writer raved about the Anheuser-Busch tour, which not only encompasses the brewery (she felt it was completely safe for kids, as her four were all under age seven), but also includes a walk over to the Clydesdale barn, which looks as spotless and decorative as something out of *House Beautiful*; a photo op with Diamond the horse and Bud the dalmatian; and a visit to the hospitality room, where adults sample beers and kids get soda and pretzels.

Whether you have children or are a couple wanting a larger tour experience, A-B offers a few different types of visits. Check out their website for more information and to see photos of this pretty spectacular-looking campus, er, estate. Hours and dates are seasonal, so check before you go. Bring your cameras, you are urged, and it's completely ADA accessible. Oh, and it's free!

Beara Irish Brewing Company

2800 Lafayette Road
Portsmouth, NH 03801
www.bearairishbrew.com

I spoke with Michael Potorti and his wife Louise just after they celebrated the grand opening of their brewery. Some months later, they announced that they were serving pizza at the taproom and looking for suggestions for other foods to expand their menu. At the time of this writing they offered the following new beer: Bourbon B-Day Gold, a stout conditioned in Jim Beam barrels for four months.

Their story? While visiting Louise's home island off Cork, Ireland, the Potortis were impressed with the quality of the local grains and dairy. They had an idea: Why not use Irish barley malt to brew beer? And why not combine that with local, New England–grown products too? That's what Beara Brew is about. Visit them at their brewery and tasting room and tap your toes to the Irish music while drinking genuine Irish brews.

When Mike's job was outsourced, he found himself with a family and home in New Hampshire and some time on his hands. "We decided to go ahead with the brewery," he explains. "I had won two awards for a honey brown and a stout brewed with the Irish barley. My wife is from Bere Island off the Beara peninsula, off Cork. People like the beer and our Kickstarter campaign was successful. We developed the recipes and leased space and went from there. There were a lot of hurdles to get over, but we did it. We just got a distributor, so the beer can soon be found in more retail establishments." I'm even seeing Beara brews in Maine.

In addition to a minimum of four brews on tap, they also serve some light food, all made locally.

Belgian Mare Brewery

207 Gilsum Mine Road
Alstead, NH 03602
(603) 835-7801
www.belgianmare.blogspot.com

Tim Roettiger is a fisheries biologist by training, but the grind of a daily long commute eventually wore thin. What a wife he has! She suggested he open a brewery. She's not for sale, but you can visit them at their farm and say hi to their Belgian mare named Aggie and her pasture-mate Seth, a riding pony from Missouri. The chickens will greet you, too. Tim runs a wood-fired brewing system he built himself. Take a tour and taste the beers in their taproom. "We make all kinds," he says. "Pale ale, saison, lagers, and a unique beer is Head Lock Stout, similar to a spruce beer, because I use spruce tips."

In spring 2016 Tim announced his latest beer: Narrenschiff, made with dark honey and dark wheat and fermented with a German ale yeast. They don't serve food, but you can get to Keene in 20 minutes and eat at Elm City Restaurant.

Border Brewery / Border Brew Supply
224 North Broadway
Salem, NH 03079
(603) 216-9134
www.borderbrewsupply.com

After selling brewing and wine-making equipment and supplies for three years, it seemed natural for Joe Ruotolo, owner of Border Brew Supply, to go to the next level and open a brewery. Pouring since May 2013, there is always something interesting in the fermentor. Joe says, "We have a 500-square-foot tasting room where we sell growlers and flights of beer." After you taste the beers, he recommends the Tuscan Kitchen for lunch or dinner.

On tap when I checked in were Peanut Butter Stout, Sticky Paw Brown, Border IPA, Pumpkin, and VBOS. Taste the ales and go home with a kit, and join the other million home brewers in this country and make your own. They offer classes and seminars, so you can't go wrong.

Candia Road Brewing / Nepenthe Ale House
840 Candia Road
Manchester, NH 03109-5201
(603) 935-8123
www.nepentheales.com

The first nanobrewery in New Hampshire, Nepenthe Ale House is one part of "a big family-operated business," brewer Thomas Neel tells me. "We have a convenience store, brewery, and a home-brew supply shop that are all separate entities." The brewery grand opening was January

1, 2012, and within a year, Neel was telling Brandon Gee of the *Boston Globe* in an article dated February 5, 2013, "We really weren't prepared for the response. We have a four- to five-week process per batch. Once we're sold out of something, we're sold out for a few weeks."

But popularity can be a good thing. Although he admits there were a lot of mistakes in the beginning, things have come along, and the beers are getting a big following. Nepenthe Ales are brewed with style guidelines in mind but, according to Neel, "tend to blur as we bring everything together . . . We brew by our own set of merits." Try the Shire Stout (7.2% ABV), described as a "dark black stout with a creamy head you can float caps on. A roasty, sweet chocolate aroma, that matches the flavor very well. Robust and full of flavor."

Canterbury Ale Works
305 Baptist Hill Road
Canterbury, NH 03224-2509
(603) 491-4539
www.canterburyaleworks.com

Steve Allman, the self-described one-man show, is "intimately connected with the entire brewing process and every . . . beer I offer . . . [and] every beer lover that comes through the door into my super cool brewery and tasting room!" Allman offers tours, samples, growlers, and 22-ounce "bombers" of his ales, including Be Hoppy! (6.5% ABV), described as a classic hop-driven East Coast American IPA. Canterbury encourages you to bring your own food (someone actually brought fresh oysters) and notes that Fox Country Smoke House is right around the corner for cheeses, meats and jerky.

In addition to making beer, Allman grows 11 varieties of hops on his ¾-acre hops yard at Hidden Wonders Farm, with a goal of using 100 percent of his own hops by the fall of 2016. He is also experimenting with growing another 16 varieties in various test beds.

Earth Eagle Brewings
165 High Street
Portsmouth, NH 03801-3724
(603) 503-2244
www.eartheaglebrewings.com

This was one of the several stops we made on Greta the Growler Getta, aka Granite State Growler Tours (at the end of this chapter). It is a fun, funky place in an ancient colonial building in beautiful downtown Portsmouth, adjacent to the A & G Homebrew Supply store which owners Alex and Gretchen McDonald opened in 2011. When the law passed allowing nanobreweries in the state, Alex and partner Butch Heilshoren decided to go for it and start brewing.

There aren't official tours, but they have a nice, newly expanded tasting room. The food is all made in-house, with locally sourced ingredients. Selections include various types of panini, grilled cheese and other hearty sandwiches, charcuterie plates, homemade pickled eggs, and great chilis that vary with ingredients. There's more, but I can't fit it all in here. You'll just have to get to Portsmouth—which has a great cluster of craft breweries, by the way—and taste away.

The beers are made with some pretty interesting (read: bizarre) ingredients, so take a look at the descriptions of brews available on their website, which features their Facebook feed. The draft offerings have included Amarillo Dancer pale ale and Lichtenhainer sour gruit, among many others, which turn around fast. They recommend you check Facebook for daily updates on the tap list.

Elm City Restaurant & Brewery
222 West Street, Suite 46
Keene, NH 03431-2459
(603) 355-3335
www.elmcitybrewing.com

That was then: Elm City opened in December 1995 in what was a huge woolen mill that once made materials for Civil War troops. Owner

Debbie Rivest told me that she and her colleagues smoke their own salmon and that their Texas-style chili took third place in the North Conway Chilifest last year. That makes a promising, mouth-watering start to their menu, which stresses sandwiches, soups, salads, appetizers, and pub dishes. Some standouts are the salmon brined in ale, then smoked and served on a board with fresh breads and Elm City mustards, and an ale-marinated, grilled chicken breast sandwich and beer-battered onion rings.

This is now: Elm City celebrated 20 years in 2015! Debbie Rivest couldn't be happier for the success of her brewpub, the only one in the Keene area, and for the up-and-coming craft brewers springing up like crazy. "Both the restaurant business and the beer business have gotten stronger," she told me right before opening for lunch on a rainy Saturday. "People go out more, and the cooking shows on television have increased awareness about good food. In the past five years, craft beer has really taken off, and I can now source most of our food locally because of the increase in farmers. Our customers love to taste new beers, and our brewer Ben Mullett continues to bring home medal after medal for us. The chefs are having fun cooking with our beer." Yep, that chocolate stout mousse Debbie described sounds like it's calling my name.

"We always have 10 to 12 of our own beers on tap," she continued. Some of the many rotated, from their website: Keene Kolsch, a German ale, "gold in color, light body, mildly fruity with low hop bitterness"; Oatmeal Pale Ale, "light copper in color, smooth, silky body with fruity aromas and flavors"; and No Name, an IPA, "copper in color, medium body with intense hop aroma and bitterness."

I can attest to Elm City's charm. That old mill contains nice shops and a really cool bookstore. The brewpub itself is cozy and family-friendly and offers outdoor seating in season. Keene is a great little walking city set in the beautiful Monadnock region. It's worth a visit.

Flying Goose Brewpub and Grille

40 Andover Road
New London, NH 03257-5901
(603) 526-6899
www.flyinggoose.com

A great après ski spot since 1996, Flying Goose is close to Ragged and Sunapee mountains off I-89, and from the looks of their bar and dining room, I can't think of a nicer spot to warm up after a day of gliding across the snow. The Goose supplies a good portion of its own electricity with solar panels, earning a good citizen award from me. There's a Thursday concert series with various musicians and singers. The menu truly offers something for everyone: from appetizers and sandwiches to pasta and full-on entrees, along with a kids' menu and lots of desserts. Local beef and even a venison goulash round it all out.

Brewer Rik Marley creates nearly 20 beers offered on tap at the pub, and you can take a growler home with you. You might find Rik at the bar talking with customers about the beers and getting feedback. You might even luck into an informal tour with the guy who masterminds the brew.

From The Barrel Brewing Company

15 Londonderry Road, Unit 9
Londonderry, NH 03053
(603) 328-1896
www.drinkftb.com

Just an hour from Portland in Londonderry is a two-year-old venture called From The Barrel (FTB), owned by brothers Jon, Joel, and Jason Anderson. I got to have a fun conference call with the trio in the dying light of evening not long after they opened, and by the time I was done, I was thinking I'd love to get my hands on their double IPA called Elle. I mean, the clock went back, so at 4 p.m. it's really 5 p.m., right? Agreed.

Jon tells the story of their beginnings: "We opened in July 2014. Joel and Jason had been home brewing for years, and as the quality got better and better, we talked about opening our own brewery. Then when New Hampshire eased up the nano laws, we decided to go for it."

When I asked, "Do any of you still have to have day jobs?" I got a throng of guffaws. "We all still have day jobs in IT and telecommunications," Jon said. From the peanut gallery I heard, "Yeah, we have no social lives." Between them, Joel and Jason are brewing four to five times a week. "We like brewing small batches, because we can experiment a lot."

Let's get to the beers. "Most will be on the hoppier side, but we do have a porter, and our opening-day summer beer, a Kölsch, was a big hit. We have a tasting room that offers flights or growler fills and a room off of that where you can look into brewery operations. We can't serve full pints, but we can do 4 ounces of every label we have available. We usually have four to six beers there. Occasionally we have some pre-packed bottles. Our double IPA called Elle flies off the shelves, and there's Remedy Porter, and a bunch of ales we rotate. Lily, a single IPA, is one of our flagship beers."

What makes From The Barrel stand out? "The biggest thing that makes us stand out is our model. We have 12 or more standard recipes and more that rotate, so you could come in and then return a few weeks later and get different beers. We love to have people come in and talk about beer, what they like and don't like. Our space allows for hanging out."

I always have to ask, "What's a good food to have with your double IPA?" "Spicy food, hands down," Jon replied. Then from either Jason or Joel: "Burgers and pizza, everything." I should know better!

For travelers who might want lunch or dinner after a visit to FTB, the guys recommend Cask and Vine, right down the street, which promises 12 tap lines, always different, featuring local New Hampshire beers. Chef Craft has worked up a small-plates menu to emphasize best bites with the best brews and wine.

Garrison City Beerworks

455 Central Avenue
Dover, NH 03820
(603) 343-4231
www.garrisoncitybeerworks.com

Having opened in December 2014, it took Garrison City only a year to win a Best Brewery in New Hampshire award from RateBeer. Gabe

Rogers makes hop-forward beers, which don't just push the limits, "but leap over them." With his certification from the Beer Judge Certification Program and years of home-brewing and culinary experience, Gabe and cofounder Mike Nadeau (who handles business operations) have been welcomed with open arms by beer pilgrims in this seacoast town.

Gabe and Mike love pale ales, porters, Belgian ales, and wild ales, and plan to share some unique beers inspired by these styles. On their website is a cool feature from DigitalPour: an up-to-date list of all beers currently available on tap. As this book went to press they boasted cans of Citra, Anomalous, Mosaic, Illusion, and Think Tank.

Great Rhythm Brewing
105 Bartlett Street
Portsmouth, NH 03801
(603) 300-8588
www.greatrhythmbrewing.com

Scott and Kristin Thornton are the duo responsible for Great Rhythm's hophead-friendly beers. Check their Facebook page for the grand opening of their new brewery at the above address. Until then, they do have extensive distribution of Resonation Pale Ale in cans throughout New Hampshire. This popular ale is described as "crisp, clean, well-balanced by a subtle malt character, and packed with a resinous dose of American hops."

Henniker Brewing Company
129 Centervale Road
Henniker, NH 03242-3280
(603) 428-3579
www.hennikerbrewing.com

Henniker doesn't offer food or snacks, but they recommend visitors head over to Daniel's Restaurant and Pub, overlooking the Contoocook River. There you can sample five of Henniker's brews, as well as relax and dine on everything you'd want from a pub: from crab cakes and quiche to burgers and entrees. Dave Currier is the owner, and Chris Shea is the brewer at this brewery that opened in 2011. In their words: "We brew beer with real New Hampshire spirit of independence, home-town pride, and hard work. Our goal is pretty simple: to bring people together, to celebrate this quirky little town we live in, and to make a living doing something we care about."

The year-round beers are Amber Apparition, an American amber ale; Hop Slinger, an IPA; Working Man's Porter, an English-style dark ale; and Miles & Miles, a dry-hopped pale ale. Seasonals have included The Roast, a coffee stout using coffee beans from White Mountain Gourmet Coffee in Concord, New Hampshire; DH IPA, a double IPA; Artisan Ale, a Belgian-style table beer dry-hopped with Noble hops; and Hometown Double Brown, a double brown ale using 1,500 pounds of malt in each batch.

Hobbs Tavern and Brewing Co.

2415 White Mountain Highway
West Ossipee, NH 03890
(603) 539-2000
www.hobbstavern.com

Owner Ash Fischbein opened Hobbs Tavern in 2014 and is making sessionable beers that complement the menu in this converted barn. Black Sheep Cream Ale and Something Went Arye IPA are two of his beers, along with Bear Camp Brown Ale and Progeny Pilsner.

Brewer Scott Travis is the magician behind the curtain and tells me that Hobbs opened right around Easter 2014 and began serving their own beer in mid-August. "I have 25 years of home-brewing," he said, "and this is my first commercial venture. I've known Ash and the other owner for years, and chatted with them at the bar of their other business. I'd bring them my home brews. When they thought of opening Hobbs, they asked me to brew. I changed careers from being a physical therapist. The biggest change is the size of batches from 10-gallon to 200-gallon batches, which is obvious. I had recipes from my files, so I'm scaling them up with software I have. I have six beers on tap now, and we'll keep Black

Sheep on all the time. We're trying to keep the ABV close to 5% to keep them sessionable."

Chef Marbin Avilez leads the kitchen team, offering some items I like to see on any menu: oysters on the half shell, sautéed mussels, and tuna tartare. Not your average pub menu. For lunch entrees, these entice: beer-braised pork ribs, mac and cheese, turkey potpie, bangers and mash, and a yellow curry stir-fry. Dinner is seafood, steak, and some pub-type dishes. There is a kids' menu, too, as well as an option to make just about anything gluten-free.

Martha's Exchange Restaurant & Brewery
185 Main Street
Nashua, NH 03060-2701
(603) 883-8781
www.marthas-exchange.com

Martha's website contains the history of the business: An icon in downtown Nashua, Martha's has been in the Fokas family for 80 years. In the beginning it was a sweets shop, and that's still there. Over the decades different members of the family helped evolve the business, and in 1993 brothers Bill and Chris Fokas installed a microbrewery. There's even a bar from one of Al Capone's speakeasies in Chicago! The menu runs from appetizers, pizza/flatbreads, and burgers to full-blown, delicious-sounding entrees. Surf? Turf? Both? Outside seating adds extra cachet in season, and a separate function room offers private parties their own space to celebrate special occasions.

Martha's brewery produces winning beers: Awards for various styles have been flooding in steadily since 2005. Apple Brown Betty won most recently in the 2013 Great International Beer Festival in the Belgian Specialty Dark Ale category. Brewer Greg Ouellette has been wowing the locals with great beers since he arrived at Martha's in 2001. I salivated over this recent offering: MacLeod's Scotch Ale (9.3% ABV), described as "a little glass of heaven. Immortal malt and smoky caramel, a warming dose of alcohol, smooth beyond smooth, eternally inviting."

Moat Mountain Smoke House and Brewing Company
3378 White Mountain Highway (Route 16)
North Conway, NH 03860-1518
(603) 356-6381
www.moatmountain.com

Jimmy Gardner is the manager of Moat, which opened in July 2000. Smack in the middle of ski country, Moat can be your after-ski destination from several nearby mountains, including Attitash, Cranmore, Black Mountain, Wildcat, and King Pine. "We smoke a lot of the food in-house: brisket, St. Louis–style ribs, salmon, pulled pork," Gardner says. "Everything on the menu is made in-house, from the salsas to the salad dressings and sauces."

Moat sources many of its ingredients locally, and they list eight farms they are currently working with. House-smoked meats headline the menu, along with nachos, quesadilla, burgers, wood-grilled pizzas, salads, and smoked pork and brisket.

As for the beers: "We generally have core beers always on tap. The lineup can include Hoffman Weiss; Miss B's Blueberry Ale; Czech Pilsner, our take on a Bohemian-style pilsner; Iron Mike Pale Ale; Bone Shaker Brown Ale, a very malty English-style brown; and Square Tail with the flavor of coffee and chocolate. We do carry some guest taps and offer a full bar. All of the beer is available to take out in 64-ounce growlers, and there are some in 16-ounce cans in four-packs. There are some rotating seasonals available in cans."

One Love Brewery
25 South Mountain Road, Unit 4
Lincoln, NH 03251
(603) 745-7290
www.onelovebrewery.com

In September 2014 One Love Brewery split off from 7th Settlement Brewery amicably. I caught up with One Love's owner/brewer Michael Snyder the day after our first snowstorm and the clock went back an hour. Snyder, who trained at the Siebel Institute in Chicago and has been brewing since 1996, was looking forward to his new venture: "I'd been keeping my eye on an empty 11,000-square-foot building in Lincoln and finally decided that's where I wanted to relocate the brewery." Not only did he plan to brew German lagers and American-style ales on a 15 bbl system there, but a full-service restaurant, meeting space, and separate event room were also in the works.

Congratulations, Michael and Jennifer Snyder and their crew, because in 2016 One Love celebrated its one-year anniversary! This is a gorgeous facility that hosts weddings and other private events in addition to the brewery and a full-service restaurant, with chef Sam Nutting doing the honors with grilled duck panini, seared scallops, and lobster mac and cheese, among many other items. The OLB Kölsch features big on tap among guest beers.

The Portsmouth Brewery
56 Market Street
Portsmouth, NH 03801-3750
(603) 431-1115
www.portsmouthbrewery.com

Opened since 1991, the Portsmouth Brewery is New Hampshire's original brewpub and has been a rock in a city where small businesses sometimes come and go. Owned by Peter Egleston and his partner Joanne Francis, the lineage goes something like this: First there was the Northampton Brewery, then came the Portsmouth Brewery, then came Smuttynose. Egleston and Francis now own the latter two, and Egleston's sister Janet retains ownership of the western Massachusetts icon.

Great food and beer continue to attract thousands of visitors every year. Right in beautiful Portsmouth (and trust me, it wasn't always this beautiful), the brewery has a full pub-style menu with a few signature dishes that sound amazing: salmon bánh mì, pork chop marinated in brown ale, lamb burger, and mussels steamed with blonde ale are among many options. Vegetarian dishes, a kids' menu, and a late-night bar menu for when you just can't stop eating round it out.

As for the beers, they serve 250,000 pints a year! The Portsmouth Brewery attracts talented brewers, most notably for me, Tod Mott, who recently opened his own brewery (Tributary in Kittery, Maine) after years of making great brews for places such as Catamount and Harpoon. Matt Gallagher now heads up the brew team, which turns out such favorites as Downeast Cider (5.1% ABV), Cirque de Citron (7.9%), Hop Harvest 2 (5.5%), Smuttynose Bouncy House (4.3%), Smuttynose Old Brown Dog (6.7%), Smuttynose Finestkind IPA (6.9%), Pumpkin Ale (5%), Zwickel Monster (5.4%), Wild Thang (5%), Scotch Ale (8.5%), Extra Special Belgian Bitter (5.5%), and Black Cat Stout (5.5%).

The Prodigal Brewery at Misty Mountain Farm

684 Townhouse Road
Effingham, NH 03882-8533
(603) 539-2210
https://www.facebook.com/TheProdigalBrewery

Founder and brewer Paul Davis returned to his native New Hampshire after years of brewing for Castle Springs Brewery (now defunct), which made the Lucknow beers, and a stint at Trout Brook / Thomas Hooker in Connecticut. The brewery is located on a farm that was in the hands of one family for over 200 years.

Davis makes traditional German lagers with an American bent and has won over two dozen awards, including taking the bronze in the Great American Beer Festival in 2010 for Reverend Potter's Baltic Porter (7.1% ABV), described as follows: "A full flavored dark lager which owes its heritage to the influence of the dark ales of England and cool fermented in the tradition of Eastern Europe. Generously hopped for balance, this beer hides its strength well, so watch out when imbibing near that warm New England fireplace on a cold eve."

Other brews on the menu look tempting, including: Effinghamburgherbrau, Sacopee Pils, Curse of the Rye-Wolf, EffinghammerWeisse, Chocorua Kolsch, Reverend Potter's Baltic Porter, Prodigal Oktoberfest, and Prognosticator Doppelbock.

Redhook Brewery / Cataqua Public House
1 Redhook Way Pease International Tradepot
Portsmouth, NH 03801
Brewery, (603) 430-8600; restaurant, (603) 501-3237
www.redhook.com/breweries/portsmouth-brewer

Another macrobrewery, as the Brewers Association classifies it, Redhook began in a transmission shop in Seattle in the early 1980s and has grown, well, a lot. It's a big beer company now, with sophisticated tours and events. If you're in the area and want a big-brewery experience, this is it. Tours include a guided walk through the brewery, Redhook history and an explanation of how they make the beers, and a sampling session with three to four samples of beer and a souvenir pint glass. On the premises is the Cataqua Public House, serving a traditional pub menu as well as some beers that are made and served only there.

Redhook belongs to the Green Alliance and uses sustainable practices that impress. Spent grains go to local farms, food waste is composted, fryer grease is recycled, and the good-citizen list goes on.

Schilling Beer Co.
18 Mill Street
Littleton, NH 03561
(603) 444-4800
www.schillingbeer.com

Owner Jeff Cozzens sent me Schilling's story to share. In their words: "Schilling Beer Co. is a family-owned, continental European-inspired artisanal brewery. We craft lagers and ales inspired by Old World traditions using a custom 5-barrel brewing system in the North Country's oldest commercial building, a circa 1798 grist mill that we renovated in partnership with Renaissance Mills of Littleton. Head Brewer John Lenzini, a chemist, educator, linguist and former resident of Germany and Austria, began brewing in buckets in grad school in 1996."

In 2016 Schilling was turning out 750 barrels of beer a year, and they have 10 to 15 beers on tap. The brewery has two floors, both with bars, and for food there are wood-fired pizzas and charcuterie plates. Here's a beer to sip on the deck when you go: Le Nain (5% ABV), a highly sessionable Belgian-style Witbier brewed with blood orange zest.

Seven Barrel Brewery
5 Airport Road
West Lebanon, NH 03784
(603) 298-5566

That was then: In 1995 I visited Seven Barrel and had a really nice chat with the bartender, Tim Howe, whose welcoming grin still makes me smile when I look at the photo I snapped. (Back when I used black-and-white film and a Pentax K1000.) Not sure where Tim is now, but Seven Barrel is still there, and has been since 1994, with its 1896 copper decoction kettle and 60-foot-long oak-paneled bar. It was voted a favorite by my Internet friend Paula Phaneuf.

This is now: Let's lead with the beer that's going to get you there, with brewer's descriptions of a couple of Seven Barrel's year-round offerings. Quechee Cream Ale (4.5% ABV): "American classic. True to style, this beer is blond in color with a low bitterness that makes this a smooth drinking beer. It's brewed with German malt and flaked maize. It's hopped with Perle and Sterling hops to about 14 IBUs." New Dublin Brown (4.5% ABV): "Another classic with an alluringly deep rich but transparent brown color. Just bitter enough to keep the sweet malt from being overpowering. Brewed with British malts and hopped with Perle, English Goldings and Willamette hops to about 20 IBUs."

The menu is heavily pub food, but with some additions to keep it interesting: cottage pie, bangers, wings, sandwiches. Then you've got some nice changeups like madras chicken on a pita, cock-a-leekie soup, roast salmon, and my favorite fantasy food, poutine.

Smuttynose Brewing Company

105 Towle Farm Road
Hampton, NH 03842
(603) 436-4026
www.smuttynose.com

In 2015 Smuttynose built a new brewery that is absolutely stunning. Get there. Meantime, let me present you with beer blogger Brian Carey's love letter to the New England beer he can't get out of his mind. Now living in Texas, Carey (whose Great Beer Now blog can be found at www.great beernow.com) once tasted Smuttynose beer and fell hard:

> *I took a vacation to the Boston area many years ago to seek out new scenery and brush up on my American history. I had never visited the New England states before and I planned to drive through all six of them over the course of about ten days, soaking up the scenery and visiting the places so important to the founding of our republic.*
>
> *Reliving America's past might have been one of the key reasons for my choice of vacation spot, but it wasn't the only one. I knew the New England states were renowned not just for history, but also for beer, and I made it a point to visit the well-known breweries in the area and sample beer from lesser-known breweries and brewpubs. I came across some beer from a New Hampshire brewery named Smuttynose and decided it was worth a try. The name "Smuttynose" sounded amusing and the beer styles available ranked among my favorites. I immediately fell in love with the beer brewed by this Hampton, New Hampshire, operation and I couldn't wait to tell everyone about my discovery when I returned home.*
>
> *I thoroughly enjoyed each of the beers I sampled, which included Smuttynose Shoals Pale Ale, Finestkind IPA, and Old Brown Dog. The pale ale was a solid entry for the style and the Old Brown Dog was about as American as a brown ale could be, with a sweetness level and nutty/roasty character that made it stand out in a crowd. But the beer I was most impressed with was Finestkind IPA. Its golden color was different from most other IPA I had sampled at the time and I liked the fact that it was well-hopped, but didn't go to extremes. I*

also appreciated the complexity of the flavors. More than just another spicy, hop-forward IPA, Finestkind was a thinking person's beer and I continued to taste and name different flavors with each sip.

Smuttynose Brewing is more widely distributed today than it was when I visited the New England area. Its beer just became available, much to my delight, in my current home state of Texas in 2014. There are other fine products brewed in the New England states, but Smuttynose ranks as my favorite and with recently established local distribution, I won't need another history-refresher vacation to satisfy my cravings for this amazing beer.

Squam Brewing Company

118 Perch Pond Road
Holderness, NH 03245-5234
(603) 236-9705
www.squambrewing.com

Owner and brewer John Glidden described Squam in a phone call with me as follows: "I make a variety of beers to appeal to all kinds of beer drinkers," he said. "We do seasonals like winter wheat, and others are rotated in and out depending on what I'm in the mood to make. I was a home brewer for quite some time, then I decided to get licensed. I'm a one-man operation, so I strongly urge people to call ahead for a tour. I don't do growlers but can sell 22-ounce bottles. My number-one-selling beer is my Golden IPA, then they like my stout and barleywine." John recommends visiting his website for contact information to arrange tours, which are $10 per person and include a pint glass and samples.

Stark Brewing Company

500 North Commercial Street
Manchester, NH 03101-1151
(603) 625-4444
www.starkbrewingcompany.com

Stark Brewing Company originally started back in 1994 as the Stark Mill Brewery. After a re-branding in 1999, it became Milly's Tavern, named after the owner's German shepherd. In 2015 Milly's again underwent a change and became Stark Brewing Company.

Owner Peter Telge appeared in 2014 on WMUR-TV and cooked up a dish he likes to serve at the brewpub: drunken chicken salad. It looks like a unique and healthy dish, with the chicken being sautéed in Stark's pumpkin ale (made using 400 pounds of roasted pumpkin), then put atop a bed of greens, onions, walnuts, cooked beets, cucumbers, tomatoes, and nice chunks of goat cheese. Light lunch means more beer! The menu is classic pub fare with some signature dishes like the chicken salad mentioned above and lamb kabobs, baked kibbee, and brewhouse chili and beef stew, both made with Milly's Oatmeal Stout. They also do some gluten-free dishes and have a Sunday brunch menu.

Stark began canning beer in the fall of 2014. With 19 taps, the brewpub can showcase the brewery's creations quite proudly, including 2013 Great International Beer Festival gold medal winner, Bo's Scotch Ale (9.5% ABV), described as follows: "A traditional scotch ale, caramel and malt sweetness dominates the palate. A full bodied ale that's higher in alcohol content than most, making it a great after dinner sipper, but definitely not for the mild at heart."

Peter Telge's plans to expand his brewery, adding more fermenting tanks and taking his beers to a national distribution level, have all come to fruition! He lit up when he talked about his hop bomb beer he calls Hop Freakin' Ridiculous, which clocks in with 220 IBUs, saying, "It's a little bitter, but well balanced." And what sets his beers apart from the others? "I make beers that blow people away," he said, noting that his oatmeal stout won gold in the World Beer Cup.

Throwback Brewery

121 Lafayette Road, Unit 3
North Hampton, NH 03862-6400
(603) 379-2317
www.throwbackbrewery.com

A tour on Greta the Growler Getta (later in this chapter) got me to Throwback on the Ides of March, a day when you're so sick of winter in central Maine that it's easy to mistake southern New Hampshire for Florida. Ides of March didn't work out so well for Julius Caesar, but there was nothing but positive vibes on this beer tour.

Started with a eye toward creating beers using 100 percent locally sourced ingredients, Throwback's owners Annette Lee and Nicole Carrier are committed to walking the walk of reducing their carbon footprint (sorry . . . pun . . . sorry). They work with local maltsters (malt farmers), and with the Northeast Hop Alliance, they hope to soon get all of their hops locally. "Beer-oir" is their term for *terroir*, the flavor of foods and drink that comes from where it's grown—the soil, the water, even the air—and that's what they are determined to achieve.

Bon Appétit magazine included Throwback on its list of 10 favorite nanobreweries. This is a fun crew and a great place to visit, and their beers continue to collect praise from all quarters.

Tuckerman Brewing Company

66 Hobbs Street
Conway, NH 03818-1058
(603) 447-5400
www.tuckermanbrewing.com

Tuckerman was opened in 1998 by Nik Stanciu and Kirstin Seves, and in November 2014 they celebrated the grand opening of their new facility. Kirstin called me and gave me the lowdown on their brewery: "Tuckerman Ravine is a bowl formed by glaciers, and with the wind patterns and weather, the snow gets blown into a bowl-like formation. So since the 1930s people have been backcountry skiing. You have to hike in and it's terrifying. We're about 20 miles south of there.

"We moved our location, just across the parking lot. We bought an empty building and had the equipment installed. We opened our tasting room and retail center in mid-November. This expands our tasting room and ability to open more often, especially during ski season. We'll be offering food soon, probably in the summer. Our head brewer is Seth Reidy, and production manager is Dave Blackburn. Currently our beers consist of a pale ale and Altbier year-round. With our new location we can do more specialty releases: an IPA, a Kölsch, and a high-strength brown ale. We'll be able to test a bunch of new recipes and give the brewers some elbow room to brew new styles."

If you travel to Conway to taste the beer, there are plenty of restaurants available for lunch or dinner. Kirsten says Tuckerman can be found in most of those places. "We're excited to have a hop garden planted in a two-acre piece of land out back. Our beers are bottle-conditioned, and they have been since 1998."

White Birch Brewing
1339 Hooksett Road
Hooksett, NH 03106-1847
(603) 244-8593
www.whitebirchbrewing.com

Opened in 2009, White Birch Brewing provides, in their words, "beers that range from historical, [to] contemporary, to the avant-garde, each batch of beer is . . . brewed by hand, and left unfiltered for an exceptional depth of flavor." When I checked their Facebook page, White Birch had a special posted: 50 percent off their Belgian Style Pale Ale and Nyx. See why social media check-ins are mandatory? People are drinking up the beer all over, as they are now distributing in cans in New Hampshire, Massachusetts, Maine, Connecticut, New York, Virginia/DC, and Maryland/Delaware.

Woodstock Inn Station & Brewery
135 Main Street
North Woodstock, NH 03262-0118
(603) 745-3951
www.woodstockinnnh.com

Peggy and Scott Rice are the proud owners of this ancient inn, which Scott saved from its abandoned state in 1982. The enterprise has grown to include the Woodstock Inn; its Woodstock Station restaurant (the actual railroad station moved to the inn's premises), with an eight-page breakfast menu and award-winning sticky buns; a brewery; and not one, but four pubs.

Butch Chase heads up the brewing operations with a 30-barrel system, making Pig's Ear Brown Ale, Grand National Champion for brown ales at the US Beer Tasting Championships in 2004 and 2006, as well as a bunch of other North Country–named gems. In their most recent renovation, they added a function space and do weddings and gatherings. Manager Erin Marley brought me up to speed: "We have a general store, and are in the midst of renovating a couple other houses to have more space. We do tours every day at noon for $5, and we encourage people to sign up the day before because they're so popular. Each person gets a pint glass and tasting after the tour. We're one-stop shopping for food, lodging, and entertainment." And, of course, beer.

New Hampshire Beer Bus Tour

Granite State Growler Tours
45 Lafayette Road
North Hampton, NH 03862
(603) 964-0284
www.nhbeerbus.com

Climb aboard "Greta the Growler Getta" and you not only get a tour of some of seacoast New Hampshire's craft breweries, you also get a lot of history lessons of the area, the players, and the beer from host Mark Chag. Co-owner Dave Adams drives and brings the homemade pretzels; Mark entertains. It's a great tour.

Each tour consists of three or four breweries in Portsmouth and Hampton, with tastings included in the ticket price plus snacks and prizes provided by local businesses. They do a few different types of tours, so check out their website for details.

Rhode Island

EVERY SCHOOLCHILD WHO HAS HAD A GEOGRAPHY LESSON KNOWS THAT Rhode Island is our nation's smallest state. But did you know it has the longest name? State of Rhode Island and Providence Plantations is the exact name of what some dub "Little Rhody." It may be short on geographical area, but it's now long on the list of craft breweries and more are opening or in planning every day.

With 35 islands, some connected by bridges that seem to float right above the gorgeous ocean, Rhode Island was one of my favorite "research" destinations when I visited there. I stayed with an old high school friend in Tiverton, then traveled all over the state to track down as many brewers as I could in a too-short, three-day trip. Next time, I'll jump on the beer bus here and get in more stops. And then there are the festivals, where you get a lot of bang for the buck. It's a beautiful place with beautiful beers!

Bucket Brewery
100 Carver Street
Pawtucket, RI 02860
www.bucketbrewery.com

Five guys teamed up and put their home-brewing skills and passion to work to create Bucket, and within a couple of years moved into a much larger facility and a 10 bbl system. They have a Kitchen Blog on their website, with lots of recipes for dishes that go well with their beers. Nate, Erik, T. J., Drew, and Ron are the Bucket crew and offer the following beer, among others: B.O.G. Cranberry-Orange Saison (5% ABV), described as "light, tart and refreshing. This subtle take on a fruit beer hints at orange zest and cranberries, and is the prefect refresher for a summer day."

When I checked in a while ago, Bucket was offering a free pint of beer to anyone who contributed a dollar to the Save the Bay (Narragansett) effort. It was a limited-time offer, but it shows the commitment many brewers have not only to their business, but to the larger world around us.

Coddington Brewing Company
210 Coddington Highway
Middletown, RI 03842-4884
(401) 847-6690
www.coddbrew.com

I landed at Coddington right after they opened for lunch one cold, blustery day. My cellphone battery had already died, and the more-than-friendly hostess offered to plug in my charger right at her station, assuring me a fresh phone for the rest of my day. It was early, so I sipped a few tastes of the beers while chatting with the bartender, who had been working there for years. In fact, Coddington was getting ready to celebrate their 19th year in business.

This place has a great "feel" to it. The bar is separated from the dining room by a partial wall, so it feels cohesive and there's a flow to the rooms. All ages trooped in for lunch, and the manager, Billy Christy, assured me that they see people there from age 4 to 94. With a pool table and flat-screen TVs, the bar is casual and friendly. The restaurant itself is immaculate and warm.

Marshall Richter, the brewer, wasn't on duty that day, but I got to step into his workplace, visible from the dining room through a huge plate-glass window, to take some photos. They keep seven of their beers on tap and another four rotate. They make an IPA, a blueberry ale, a golden ale, and a stout. Billy told me they are branching out and that their imperial stout went over really well.

The menu is a large one, offering appetizers like a spicy calamari with banana peppers (ouch) and clams casino, along with the usual pub fare of wings, nachos, and dips. Then there are pizzas, sandwiches (including a lobster roll), salads, and entrees like pasta, baked and fried seafood, steaks, and ribs. This is a real family-friendly brewpub with a super-efficient and friendly staff.

Foolproof Brewing Company

241 Grotto Avenue
Pawtucket, RI 03860-3403
(401) 721-5970
www.foolproofbrewing.com

The day I spoke with him, Nick Garrison, owner of Foolproof, was headed up to Worcester, Massachusetts, for a "ride-along" where he'll visit some accounts with a salesperson from his distributor. "I'm trying to visit key accounts," he said. "They like to meet owners of breweries that are not in their neighborhood. I've heard Worcester is up-and-coming, mirroring Providence, and its beer market is roughly the same size as the state of Rhode Island. Our beers are available statewide in Rhode Island, Connecticut, and Massachusetts. We launched the company about 18 months ago." Making beer is more than just brewing. Marketing and distribution are key, as Nick has found out.

"The genesis for the idea of Foolproof happened when people complimented me on the beer I had made and served at my wedding, not knowing I'd brewed it. The proverbial lightbulb went off. I was in the aerospace industry and started brewing at that time. We have a brewmaster, a chemist by trade, and he does the production part of the business. I'm doing the business part."

When I asked Nick's take on what foods to pair with his beers, he said, "One of my favorites is our saison paired with oysters on the half shell—they are a super combination—and Raincloud with vanilla ice cream in the beer. A basic one I love is a cheeseburger with our Backyahd, our quintessential New England BBQ beer."

Nick continued, "I like the way we think about our beer. We pair our beer with life. It's a concept that's resonated with beer-lovers. Experiences like flipping burgers, going to a baseball game, and even getting married, those are the times we associate with beer."

"It's your life, your beer" is the tagline of this Pawtucket beer company that has a philosophy of "experience-based brewing," making beer to savor for each experience its drinker is having at the time. Interesting concept, and my friend Nate Byrnes must agree, since he waxes positively poetic about their Russian imperial stout, Foolproof Raincloud Revery:

As black and slick as motor oil, Foolproof's Revery is by far the strongest brew produced by the highly promising Pawtucket brewery. Despite clocking in at an eye-blurring 10.7% ABV, this beast of a Russian imperial stout (RIS) meows like a kitten, as the expected alcohol flavor is nowhere to be found. Revery can easily cause alcohol-induced reverie as one loses mental focus under the haze of a good buzz.

Instead of alcohol heat, the drinker is treated to a complex series of flavors. Rich and thick, Revery treats the tongue to a cornucopia of tastes. From a variety of darkly roasted malts, to cocoa, to roasted oats and caramel, the beer slides through the mouth with a velvety, constantly shifting wave of flavors. The kaleidoscope of flavors is both intricate and subtle, showing brewmaster Damase Olsson's skilled craftsmanship. Foolproof uses a blend Northern Brewer, Tettanger, and Hallertau hops both to balance the massive malt profile that the style demands AND to add trace spice and earth aromas and flavors to the beer. The end product is a magnificently balanced brew.

Grey Sail Brewing of Rhode Island
63 Canal Street
Westerly, RI 02891
(401) 212-7592
www.greysailbrewing.com

Jen and Allan Brinton own this coastal brewery, which brewed its first beer on November 11, 2011. Jen spoke with me on a summer day, when her praise of Westerly's beauty made me envious. I could picture the old fort, the sailboats plying the blue-green water, the beaches at Watch Hill, the saltwater pond and Victorian strolling park. What's not to entice? Add a brewery to that scenery, and it's a win-win for everyone.

"My husband, Allan, had plans to open a brewery or brewpub for a long time," Jill said. "Finally, on our 10th wedding anniversary, I committed to that dream with him. Once we made the decision, it went very quickly. Things fell into place. I run the business end, and with four children, it's a challenge. I'm available to them all day, and sometimes I'm doing computer work at 3 a.m. Allan keeps his full-time job as a chemical engineer. We decided to adopt the motto 'We are not employing ourselves here,' so we have a core staff and a head brewer, Josh LeTourneau. It's not technically employee-owned, but the staff owns a percentage of the business. Allan and I are here on weekends, so when people come in for a tour, they are meeting the owners. We really enjoy pouring the beer and talking with people. We do hand-drawn casks, and Josh is always brewing up something wonderful and new."

Josh LeTourneau worked at Mayflower Brewing in Plymouth, Massachusetts, for two-plus years, then went over to Grey Sail as head brewer. Josh told me, "The Rhode Island craft beer movement is blossoming, and we're trying to be on the leading edge of it." He happily listed some of the beers they make: "We have a cream ale and EPA [extra pale ale] that Allan wanted to open with. For the seasonals, he wanted to do a smoked porter and I chose one of my favorite styles, a Belgian. We'll do a pumpkin this fall. I'm willing to try to brew anything. I like the creativity of it. That's the fun of it, gets me back to my home-brewing roots, where you wake up on a Saturday and brew whatever you want. Recipe development is really fun."

Grey Sail made a deep impression on beer fan and blogger Eric Ciocca, a native of Westerly:

Grey Sail started with two flagship beers—"ship" being the obvious motif in their nautical label design. Their Flying Jenny XPA (6% ABV, 54 IBU) and Flagship cream ale (4.9% ABV, 22 IBU) are light by today's hop-heavy standards, but when introduced they were a pleasant deviation from the mainstream. Designed to be beach- and boat- friendly, Grey Sail adopted the can format back when other brewers were scratching their heads in indecision. Having smuggled a six-pack of this to my favorite secret seawall, I found that these beers are a nice addition to any sun-soaked and sandy adventure. They are not intrusive, sweet enough to be present, crisp enough to cut through a parched thirst, and light enough so you feel like you can go swimming immediately after finishing one without waiting the mom-proscribed 30 minutes.

Today Grey Sail offers a number of seasonal and occasional one-off beers. I would be doing a disservice if I didn't immediately mention their Captain's Daughter, a double IPA (8.5% ABV, 69 IBU) that does not skimp on the hops. It has a tropically fruity nose that draws you in, a profile that at the same time keeps you mindful that it is a DIPA while not punishing you for it, and a signoff that leaves you wanting another sip. This is a great beer to pair with a sweet and creamy dessert, or just to enjoy slowly while you read. It is engaging from start to end, and packs a punch that reminds you of your first glass even as you are considering a second.

Grey Sail's Hazy Day Belgian wit (4% ABV, 20 IBU) is a summer offering that hits markets in the late spring. I associate it with windy days, full sails, and the first time in the year you can walk outside without a jacket. It is light with a bit of cereal flavor. Comparable to an Allagash White, but a head above Blue Moon, this beer can be enjoyed with or without an orange slice garnish. It is a nice pairing with a plate of bread and cheese, a reasonable substitute for a dry white wine.

The winter seasonal, Leaning Chimney stout (6% ABV, 34 IBU), is named after the now-crooked brick chimney placed inconveniently in the middle of the brewery. The owners mentioned the possibility of having it removed, but like the rest of the building it remains as part of the characteristic charm. The beer is smoked but not overly so. You might not even pick up on the peaty rauchbier notes depending on the pour and shape of glass—it's all in the head. The base of the beer is roasty and chocolately. It doesn't have an abundance of milky sweetness that I favor in a stout, but it is drinkable and side-steps the bitterness sometimes found in porter-style stouts. It's a great beer to curl up with on a cold winter night.

Mohegan Cafe & Brewery
213 Water Street
Block Island, RI 02807
(401) 466-5911
www.mohegancafebrewery.com

You have to take the ferry or an airplane to Block Island. If you aren't a descendant of the silver spoon crowd and take the ferry, Mohegan Cafe & Brewery is located right there, across from where you get off. How convenient! The menu is extensive and you can enjoy pub fare, full-on entrees, burgers, or get that eleventy-seventh lobster roll, I dare you. David Sniffen is the on-premise brewmaster. I bet his Mohegan Pilsner would go great with that clam chowder and the aforementioned lobster roll. There is a lengthy wine list, too, and cocktails.

Narragansett Brewing Company
461 Main Street
Pawtucket, RI 02860
(401) 437-8970
www.narragansettbeer.com

In an open letter to Narragansett drinkers in April 2016, CEO Mark Hellendrung announced that 'Gansett was building out a new brewery in Pawtucket. "Several months will be spent restoring the building and installing the brew house, and later this year, we'll be brewing 'Gansett in the Ocean State for the first time since 1983." Local again.

Founded in 1890, Narragansett is New England's oldest beer, celebrating its 125th anniversary in 2015. It was the No. 1 beer in New England from the 1890s through the 1970s and was the official beer of the Red Sox for over 30 years. It's the first beer I tasted, begging a sip from my dad on a summer Saturday as he settled in at his place at the table with a crossword puzzle, a plate of saltines covered with squares of American cheese, and Ned Martin (or was it Curt Gowdy?) on the radio, broadcasting the game. Welcome back, neighbor!

Newport Storm Brewery
293 J. T. Connell Road
Newport, RI 02840
(401) 849-5232
www.newportstorm.com

Newport Storm is right down the road from the Coddington Brewing Company brewpub, so you can combine a brewery tour and tasting with lunch or dinner afterward. The day I visited, I found a bustling tasting room on a weekday at noon, a good sign that word is out about the beers and the tour. I didn't hit a guided tour, but the observation deck has a self-guided tour complete with placards and photos that show the time line and history of the brewery, from the college days of the four founders—all of whom graduated from my alma mater, Colby College—to the present. It's quite extensive, and when you look below, you can see everyone at work. That day they were bottling.

The tasting room is warm and welcoming, and there you can buy a wide variety of styles and flavors of brews. My favorite is the India Point Ale (6.5% ABV), which is made with Rhode Island–grown hops and named after India Point in Providence. Into spirits? Try their Thomas Tew rum. Oh, ho ho.

Ravenous Brewing Company
840 Cumberland Hill Road
Woonsocket, RI 03895
(401) 216-5331
www.ravenousbrew.com

Dorian Rave and Chris Combs are wowing their customers with their acclaimed Coffee Milk Stout, among other brews. Ravenous is a nanobrewery, "on the small side," as one Yelp reviewer said, and that makes it cozy. The duo also gives back, as many do, by pouring at events like Pints for Paws, with money going to the Providence Animal Rescue League. And among the sweetest gestures I've seen in a long time, Dorian created a sessionable IPA for his wife, who had just had a baby. Sarah IPA has a blend of Chinook, El Dorado, and Cascade hops and comes in at a very drinkable 4.7% ABV. See what you learn by checking the Facebook page? Truly handy when a phone call just isn't possible—I think they're washing kegs, or brewing, or both!

Revival Brewing Co. at Brutopia

505 Atwood Avenue
Cranston, RI 02920
(401) 372-7009
www.revivalbrewing.com
www.brutopiabrewery.com

Let's clarify: Revival is brewed at Brutopia and shares the same address. Brutopia is a BBQ-inspired brewpub where you can enjoy 15 taps of Sean Larkin's beers, some created for Brutopia and served there. All the same great brewing talent shows up in both Brutopia's and Revival's beers. And suit up for BBQ, courtesy of pit-master Richard Benson.

Now for Revival's story: Led by veteran brewer Sean Larkin and his partners, Revival has been voted best brewery in Rhode Island a few times. Larkin has brewed at Trinity and consulted for Narragansett and is currently brewing Revival beers at Brutopia, a brewpub in Cranston. In the realm of the crazy-busy, this team is the very definition. But I managed to reach CEO Owen Johnson one gray day when we were getting a "wintery mix."

With a background as a home brewer and a startup expert, Owen put heads together with Sean. "We began planning Revival, combining our passions for brewing," he said. "Our third cofounder, Jeff Grantz, is our creative director. We collaborate using Sean's industry knowledge, and he comes up with the types of beers he thinks people will want; then the rest of us use our expertise to get it to everyone. We brew in two locations: Cottrell and at Brutopia."

Owen wants you to know, "We are really focused on creating craft beer that's accessible to everyone, from hardcore craft enthusiasts to the big beer drinker." Their flagship, which debuted in 2011, is Double Black IPA, described here: "The heavy roast profile of our Double Black IPA is accented by an explosion of hops. Tones of coffee, vanilla, wood and citrus mix with herbal notes to make this beer the complex beast that it is." Check the website for more of the wizard Larkin's brews.

Trinity Brewhouse
186 Fountain Street
Providence, RI 02903-1813
(401) 453-2337
www.trinitybrewhouse.com

Trinity is one of the originals in Rhode Island, and their beers have been winning awards since 1997. Located close to just about every event venue in Providence, this place makes a perfect pre- or post-concert or movie destination. How does this sound: "Stout and Teriyaki Steak Tips—Black angus steak tips, marinated in garlic teriyaki and our house stout, seared with bell peppers and oven roasted tomato, served over aromatic white rice"? Classic pub fare like pizzas, burgers, and appetizers are rounded out with some interesting entrees, like the steak tips and pilsner-steamed mussels. Eight of their own beers are on tap, including prize-winner Redrum Red Ale. That would make Stephen King proud.

Union Station Brewery
36 Exchange Terrace
Providence, RI 02903-1798
(401) 274-2739
www.johnharvards.com

Union Station was Rhode Island's first brewpub and is a member of the fine John Harvard's Brewery and Ale House family. Since 1993 they have brewed and served their own handcrafted beer alongside classic American tavern fare in this former Union Station train depot. A rotating selection of seasonal and specialty brews is available, including nonalcoholic root beer and cream soda, and all the food is made from scratch.

On a cold November evening, as I scanned their menu online, I wanted to call to ask if they delivered . . . to Maine. Here's what got me salivating: Loaded Kettle Chips, with cheddar cheese, bacon, scallions, and sour cream. Alas, they don't deliver, but next time I visit the Ocean State, I'll make this a definite stop. I think I'll try the 2013 gold medal winner in the World Beer Championship, Oktoberfest, with them chips. And you know when a restaurant has been around for over 20 years, it's doing something right.

Whalers Brewing Company

Pallisades Mill
1070 Kingstown Road, #101
Wakefield, RI 02879
(401) 284-7785
www.whalersbrewing.com

I found Whalers in the beautiful old stone mill on a blustery April day when I thought spring was here, but discovered it clearly was not! This was a magical Pied Piper experience: I had to walk from one end of the parking lot to the other to find Whalers, and along the way, I encountered two women with small children, who were also looking for the brand-new brewery. We then picked up a nice young guy who worked for a woodworker in another bay of the mill and had heard they'd acquired a new neighbor, and he joined us in our search for the elusive beer.

Our noses led us to a bay with a tiny sign taped to the door. Alas, it was locked. But being the detective I am, I noticed a box of steaming spent grains at the curb, so we knew someone was inside brewing. It was just not to be: We couldn't raise anyone to open the door. But since then, my friend Eric Ciocca and others have found their way to get the beer, and it's making an impression.

I finally connected with owner Andy Tran about six months after his brewery opened. "We started distribution on April 21, and as of last week, we're in about 12 locations and that's growing by the week," he said.

"We're lucky to be in this spot. We [Andy and partners Josh and Wes] are sons of South Kingstown and have ties to the community, and we've had an amazing amount of support. People are so happy to have the brewery here. The town council members, state reps, and congressmen have visited." As for pairing, Andy said the stout is an autumn-style beer, which goes perfectly with pumpkin pie or a creamy dessert, and even served on top of ice cream.

Here is the brewer's description of Hazelnut Cream Stout, one of Whalers' flagship beers: "This beer has generous amounts of flaked oats, chocolate malt and roasted barley giving it a complex body, creamy mouthfeel, and pours with a thick tan head. Fresh brewed hazelnut coffee is added prior to kegging. Not too heavy, not too light, this beer is perfect."

Rhode Island Beer Bus Tour
The Rhode Island Brew Bus
(401) 585-0303
www.therhodeislandbrewbus.com

Bill Nangle is a lucky guy, eliminating the usual post-college drab life of offices and neckties, and jumping into owning his own business: driving people around the Ocean State to taste beer! His company offers four formal tours, but they do private tours, too. All tickets include tastings, tours, transportation, water, snacks, games, beer education, giveaways, and pint glasses. Some tours include food, others don't. Check the website for details. Bill has a staff of five tour guides who will keep you informed and entertained. And that post-college necktie? Bill avoided that and instead wears a black T-shirt that says "Drink Rhode Island Beer."

Vermont

I ATTENDED A WRITERS' CONFERENCE A FEW YEARS AGO IN MONTPE-lier, and the drive alone is spectacular. The rolling hills are mesmerizing, and at one point, on my way home after a heady week with other writers, I was driving the only car on the road. I dipped and curved around dramatic drop-offs, my stomach dropped and my head got light, and I started laughing, all to myself. There was a moment when I thought, "This is it. This is what it's like to be 'going home.'" I felt like I was heading to heaven. Yes, that Heaven. And it felt great. Now, it's up for grabs as to whether I'll be going to Heaven, but when you pair the beers made here with the landscape, you've got heaven on earth. That's what Vermonters will tell you, anyway. My friend Chip Caton swears that Three Penny Taproom in Montpelier is a perfect place to try beers that can be hard to get elsewhere.

14th Star Brewing Company
133 North Main Street, #7
Saint Albans, VT 05478-1900
(802) 528-5988
www.14thstarbrewing.com

A brewery conceived in the imaginations of active-duty soldiers? In their words: "While deployed overseas, soldiers have plenty of time to contemplate two things: Beer and getting out of the Army. Steve and his buddies were doing just that in 2010 when the idea came to the long-time homebrewers: Why not open a brewery, preparing for the day we can retire from the Army?"

And they have realized that dream. 14th Star moved to a 16,000-square-foot facility in 2014 and sell their flagship beer, Valor Ale, in growlers, bombers, and on tap at their tasting room. Part of the proceeds of the sales of Valor, a hoppy amber ale, benefit the Purple Hearts Reunited Foundation, which returns lost or stolen medals of valor to the veterans who earned them.

A quick check-in as of this writing found great news: 14th Star got the chance to expand into an adjoining space in their strip mall location, doubling their frontage. This will allow them to host more events and will give a view into the brewery. And they announced the revival of one of their favorite beers: 1493 IPA, generously dry-hopped with citrusy hops and fresh citrus zest, on tap for a limited time. Ah, what better way to grasp the concept of impermanence than to drink beers that come and go?

The Alchemist

100 Cottage Club Road
Stowe, VT 05672
www.alchemistbeer.com

Well, well . . . In the *finally* department, I can joyously announce that The Alchemist's new brewery opened in July 2016. Fanfare! Congratulations to the gang producing one of the most sought-after beers in craft brewdom: Heady Topper. Served first at their 7 bbl brewpub in Waterbury until Hurricane Irene destroyed it, Heady was then produced on a 15 bbl system called The Cannery. Demand became so pronounced, owners Jen and John Kimmich closed the place to the public (think storming the gates—a bit dramatic on my part, but you get it—and too-long lines) and began selling it in retail shops and at pop-up sales, all the while planning, getting licensing, and building their new brewery in Stowe. There are a bona fide tasting room, tours, and, of course, a retail shop. Enjoy another gem in the crown of Vermont craft beer.

Backacre Beermakers
Weston, VT 05160
www.backacrebeermakers.com

Very interesting! More of a "blendery" than a brewery, Backacre makes a unique sour golden ale that will mature for years if stored properly. In their words: "Not a 'brewery' in the common sense of the word, Backacre Beermakers may be the first example of a 'blendery' in the United States. We work with nearby brewers to produce wort (unfermented beer) that we then take to our place for its long transformation into beer. From this stock we carefully blend a single product: Backacre sour golden ale."

When I didn't find a Facebook page for Backacre, let alone a phone number, I thought of the great folks at Three Penny Taproom in Montpelier. They must know something! They did. "Oh, yes, they are still very much in business, making the sour golden ale," Kevin at Three Penny said. Great! My friend Chip Caton raves about Three Penny, so get thee there for an amazing array of beers, or check the Backacre website for other places to find their ale in Vermont.

Bobcat Café & Brewery
5 Main Street
Bristol, VT 05443-1317
(802) 453-3311
www.thebobcatcafe.com

Celebrating over a decade as a community-supported enterprise, Bobcat has been wowing people with their beers and food—100 mug club members! Brewmaster Mark Magiera uses high-quality grains, hops, and yeast strains to create true-to-style beers. The cafe serves three of their own beers on tap and has guest taps of mostly local brews and cider. This is the type of place I wish we had more of in the smaller cities in Maine: warm, thoughtfully conceived, good local food, and homemade beer. The food is sourced as locally as possible, and the chef cooks with the seasons.

The menu features some of the most original dishes I've seen on a pub menu. Take a look at these appetizers: VT Apple Cider and Butternut

Squash Bisque with Toasted Pumpkin Seeds; Curried Chicken and Lentil Stew with Mint Pesto and Peanuts; and Kale Salad with Lemon Honey Tahini Vinaigrette. Yes, those are just a few of the apps! The entrees are tempting, too. Bristol is 30 minutes from Middlebury, so you can combine tasting trips.

Drop-In Brewing Company

610 Route 7 South
South Middlebury, VT 05753
(802) 989-7414
www.dropinbrewing.com

Brewmaster Steve Parkes has an impressive industry résumé as long as your arm, and after reading his qualifications on Drop-In's website, I'm making a beeline to Middlebury to snag some growlers of his creations. Here are his year-round offerings, but there are more rotating: Sunshine & Hoppiness (5.1% ABV), described as a "Belgian-style Golden Ale brewed with Weyermann's Malt from Germany, Cascade hops from Oregon and a blend of two Belgian yeast strains"; Heart of Lothian (5.6% ABV), a "Scottish 90 / (Shilling) Ale brewed with Scottish Golden Promise barley malt, British floor malted crystal and choco-late malts, Fuggle and Kent Golding hops, and British yeast"; and Red Dwarf (5.2% ABV), an "American Amber Ale, brewed with American 2 Row Malt, English crystal malt, Columbus, Willamette, Mt. Hood and Cascade hops, and a West Coast American yeast strain."

Drop-In's tasting room features brewing memorabilia from all over the United States. Steve and his wife, Christine, are living the dream.

Fiddlehead Brewing

6305 Shelburne Road
Shelburne, VT 05482-4437
(802) 399-2994
www.fiddleheadbrewing.com

Brewmaster and owner Matt Cohen—or Matty O, as he's called—makes beer for the true connoisseur, offering seasonals and specialty brews in the taproom and his flagship Fiddlehead IPA on draft all over Vermont. Samples at the taproom are free, and you can take home either a growlette (32 ounces) or a growler (64 ounces).

The list of beers Matty O makes and has made is so long, it'd be impossible to reproduce it here. But there is some serious alchemy going on at Fiddlehead. One brew in particular caught my eye. Matty O and colleague Rachel Cleveland collaborated with 80 breweries all over the world to make Boosa, a medium-bodied pale ale. The event was spearheaded by the Pink Boots Society, an organization that works to support the role women play in the craft beer industry today.

I have the worst timing in the world, so when tasting room wrangler Ryan took time out to talk to me on a getting-busy-fast Saturday, I was happy to get some news: "We pour our IPA year-round. The other two taps we keep rotating. Twice monthly we have new beers to sample. We started canning in the last six months, and we're soon releasing Second Fiddle, our DIPA. We like to do side projects like barrel-aging, brew for charity events, attend brewfests. We love to partake in community events." Thanks, Ryan!

Foley Brothers Brewing Company
79 Stone Mill Dam Road
Brandon, VT 05647-9612
(802) 465-8413
www.neshoberiverwinery.com

Foley Brothers Brewing is part of the family-run Neshobe River Brewing Company, Neshobe River Winery, and the Inn at Neshobe River. This is another trifecta: brewing beer, making wine, and offering refuge at a bed-and-breakfast, all in one place. I talked to patriarch Bob Foley and almost made a reservation. That'll have to wait a bit, but how can you go wrong with that combo? The tasting room is in a 19th-century barn. Bob told me that their new beer, Fair Maiden, a double IPA, had just been given a 95 rating by Beer Advocate and was at number 62 in the country.

A check-in revealed a beer called Black Heart, which is aged in Kentucky Bourbon barrels. Foley also participates in beer-related events and pairing dinners, so check the Facebook page for updates.

Four Quarters Brewing

150 West Canal Street, Suite 1
Winooski, VT 05404
www.fourquartersbrewing.com

Four Quarters celebrated their second anniversary in 2016, and Brian Eckhert is brewing some interesting beers. A note on their website "wishlist" asked for people to let him know where he could acquire *Rosa rugosa* petals to use in a saison to be named after his daughter, Juniper Rose. This was a new ingredient to me, but those are my favorite wild early-summer blooms, especially when I see them waving in a slight breeze by the ocean.

On January 16, 2015, Eckhert was honored by Ethan Fixell in *Food & Wine* magazine's blog FWx (www.foodandwine.com/fwx) in a post titled "Meet the Man Running the Best Little Brewery You've Never Heard Of." Fixell asks Eckhert about the more than 20 different beers he had brewed up until the interview. Eckhert reveals that saison is one of his favorite styles and goes on to talk about how he came up with a whiskey sour beer after a friend who doesn't like beer sent him a photo of a whiskey sour cocktail. He was working on getting sushi into the taproom, too. Sushi and beer and a drive to Vermont, anyone?

Harpoon Brewery–Vermont

336 Ruth Carney Drive
Windsor, VT 05089-9419
(802) 674-5491
www.harpoonbrewery.com/breweries/windsor

Let's just say this: When I called the Vermont location of Harpoon, the tasting room was so busy and loud, the person who answered the phone could hear nothing of what I said. I heard a lot of enviable jostling and fun-having by the Saturday brewery-goers. Nothing speaks volumes about success than, well, volume. The Harpoon Riverbend Taps and Beer Garden, located in the same building as the brewery, offers a full selection of Harpoon beers along with food to pair with your pint. Take a guided tour of the brewery on Friday, Saturday, or Sunday. Check the website, though, because they might close for a holiday or two.

Hermit Thrush Brewery
29 High Street, Suite 101C
Brattleboro, VT 05301
(802) 257-2337
www.hermitthrushbrewery.com

I was having my 19th nervous breakdown as I perused www.vtbeer .org, owned and written by Jim Welch, and saw that this new brewery opened when my first-draft deadline loomed. As I put in the final edits, I am happy to report that Hermit Thrush has been up and running at the hands of its creators, Christophe Gagne and Avery Schwenk. While Christophe brews his beloved Belgian-inspired ales, like Green St. Sour IPA, Avery takes care of "lateral thinking." I think that means he runs the business. Seriously, though, the beers are getting good reviews. When I checked in on their social media sites, on their list of beers was a saison aged in Stonecutter Spirits gin barrels. Shaken or stirred?

Hill Farmstead Brewery
403 Hill Road
Greensboro Bend, VT 05842-8813
(802) 533-7450
www.hillfarmstead.com

"Hill Farmstead Brewery Named Best Brewery in the World 2013." That was the headline in an article published in *Craft Beer* in February 2013 about the honor bestowed on Hill Farmstead by RateBeer, "the world's largest, most popular beer review website." Not only did RateBeer's members and experts choose this brewery and their beers, but regular old beer-lovers are regaling me with their own raves about them.

The lines are long for growler fills, so plan ahead. And if you can't get there in person, or don't want to wait, sample the beers at the Three Penny Taproom in Montpelier. I hear good things about this beer bar from Chip Caton of Connecticut, who loves to ski in Vermont and sample beers everywhere he schusses.

On a muggy summer morning, I talked with Shaun Hill, owner and brewer, who built the brewery on land that has been in the family for generations. In his words: "Around 1999 I wanted to open a brewery on family land that had been owned by other Hill family. I have very little documentation because there was a fire and the town hall burned, and a lot of records were lost. Our family genealogist passed away, and he was our last link. But I do know Aaron Hill moved from Greensboro proper to North Greensboro in 1803, and he opened this tavern, on a highway between Montpelier and Canada."

With an enormous expansion now complete, Hill Farmstead welcomes visitors. In May 2016 they debuted a beer called Art. Here's the brewer's description: "Art is the wine barrel-fermented and aged version of Arthur (1922–2005), our grandfather's youngest brother as well as the name of our rustic farmstead ale. In honor of Arthur, we mindfully blend his namesake beer from French oak wine barrels that have been aged and conditioned for between 1 and 3 years." Their beers are very popular and, they say, extremely limited. The most extensive draft selection is available at the brewery, which features six to eight draft lines and limited-release bottles. Check the website before you make the long journey.

Idletyme Brewing Company
1859 Mountain Road
Stowe, VT 05672
(802) 253-4765
www.idletymebrewing.com

In November 2015 restaurateurs Michael and Laura Kloeti bought Crop Bistro and changed the name from Crop Bistro & Brewery to Idletyme Brewing Company. Before it was Crop this place was The Shed, which was a beloved—and that's not too dramatic a term—local brewpub. And that's what the Kloetis hope to make it once again.

Brewmaster Will Gilson is still making his great beers and works with the kitchen to come up with dishes such as Idletyme Pale Ale–battered fish or tofu (yes, I said beer-battered tofu) and chips; an onion tart made with Gilson's Helles Brook Lager; and a vanilla porter sticky-toffee pudding. There is an outstanding outdoor Biergarten in season that is also dog-friendly. My blogger friend Hophead wrote from his visit there that "it was six for six with the beer flight." Batting a thousand!

Watch some of the website's mini-videos of Will's shenanigans in the brewery. I can't wait to try that stout he poured in one of them. Here's the brewer's description: "British-style Oatmeal Stout—5.2% ABV. Invitingly smooth, clean and full-bodied. Roasted malt in mouth, finishes with coffee and chocolate notes. Excellent any time of the year."

Kingdom Brewing
353 Coburn Hill Road
Newport, VT 05855-9915
(802) 334-7096
www.kingdombrewingvt.com

Here is another enterprising husband-and-wife team, Brian and Jenn Cook, who not only run a farm where they raise Angus cattle, but brew beer. Visit Brian and Jenn; pet the cows, who love the spent grain, hops, and yeast, according to Brian; and pick up some veggies for dinner. Their flagship beer is Out of Bounds, described as "strong with a smoother mouth feel than many with a pleasant IPA POW at the end." Check their website for what's on tap. These caught my eye: Kingdom Brown (6.8% ABV), Black River Schwarzbier (4.5% ABV), and Scottish Winter Brown (9% ABV).

Lawson's Finest Liquids
Warren, VT 05674
(802) 272-8436
www.lawsonsfinest.com

Great news for fans of Sean Lawson's beers came in 2016 when Sean and Karen Lawson announced they would buy a property in Waitsfield, Vermont, to house a 30 bbl brewery and family-friendly tasting room.

Because their current 7 bbl brewery is located in a residential area, it isn't open to receive the hordes of beer drinkers who would like to visit. This new facility will be a sip of sunshine to all craft beer lovers. Shortly after that announcement came this one: Their Maple Tripple Ale won silver in the Specialty Beer category at the 2016 World Beer Cup.

To help with supply, Lawson has been brewing in collaboration with Two Roads Brewing in Connecticut, which allows Sip of Sunshine and Super Session #2 to be kegged and distributed in Vermont and Connecticut. The new brewery and tasting room may be ready in 2017, but stuff happens. Let's all keep our fingers crossed. Check the website for updates and for places where you can find Lawson's Finest beer.

Long Trail Brewing Company

5520 US 4
Bridgewater Corners, VT 05035-0168
(802) 672-5011
www.longtrail.com

It was eons ago that Long Trail Brewing changed its name from Mountain Brewers, and I got the explanation back then from Andy Pherson, founder and president of the company: "Our Long Trail beers are better known than we are, and for years that's how most people have referred to us. We're just making it formal." What I didn't know then was that the Long Trail, the oldest long-distance hiking trail in the United States, was cut through the length of Vermont by the Green Mountain Club.

In a later interview, Andy told me that Long Trail Brewing had expanded by moving to a 9-acre campus with a 15,000-square-foot brewery, huge at the time. What has been added is a full-on tasting room with a nice pub-fare-forward food menu. Long Trail beers are now widely distributed and still loved by many.

Lost Nation Brewing
87 Old Creamery Road
Morrisville, VT 05661-6117
(802) 851-8041
www.lostnationbrewing.com

Allen Van Anda and James Griffith claim, "We who wander are not lost," reworking a line from Tolkien's *The Fellowship of the Ring*. I'm a hairs-breadth away from getting that quote on a bumper sticker and slapping it on my car! Located in northern Vermont, Lost Nation "takes inspiration from lesser known European beer styles, along with local Vermont life" to guide their brews. One of their year-round offerings is Petit Ardennes (4.2% ABV), described as "a light bodied blonde beer with notes of spice, herb, and tropical fruit. A very sessionable beer with a low alcohol content that still has great flavor."

A really nice feature the guys have on the website is a suggested food pairing with each beer. To go with the Petit Ardennes, they suggest either pork carnitas tacos or a marinated tempeh sandwich. Meat eaters and vegetarians alike will appreciate this thoughtfully prepared local food to accompany their beer.

Madison Brewing Company
428 Main Street
Bennington, VT 05201
(802) 442-7397
www.madisonbrewingco.com

I love seeing reviews where both parts of a couple love a place, for the food and for the beer. The maple barbecue wings get high marks, as does the Belgian white beer. Gluten-free does well, and one reviewer will make the long drive again to visit Madison Brewing. And lo and behold, I wrote about this very phenomenon back when I included Madison in my first edition of *What's Brewing*: "An interesting menu combines with friendly staff and designer decor to bring Bennington its first brewery restaurant. Owned and run by the Madison family—Mark, Mel, Mike, and their parents—this establishment offers some of the most interesting entrees I've seen in a 'pub.'"

Back then the menu had such items as Delmonico steak. I'm not sure anyone knows what "Delmonico" means now, but you can get burgers, wings, salads, sandwiches, bison meat loaf, cottage pie, and fish-and-chips, among many other items. The beers? There's a nice IPA, Hopback (7% ABV), that they describe as: "Our version of a bold American dry hopped IPA. Kettle hops of Apollo, Falconer's Flight and Simco. Dry hopped with Apollo and Columbus." A Yorkshire-style strong ale and a milk stout pique my interest, too.

Doing my best due diligence, I called to get an update and was told that Mike and Mel still own Madison's. That was all I got, though, from a busy chef who happened to pick up the phone on a Monday morning.

Magic Hat Brewery and Artifactory
5 Bartlett Bay Road
South Burlington, VT 05403
(802) 658-2739
www.magichat.net

Even though Magic Hat has been owned by a corporation for years, visitors rave about the brewery and the tour and the free samples you get afterward for you and your pup (yes, it's pet-friendly for "friendly dogs"). Do either the self-guided tour or arrive in time for the guided one. Call ahead if you have a group, please. But if you're in Burlington, a haven for craft beer, go on over. Magic Hat's #9 may have been your gateway to the craft brew world, so visit an old friend.

McNeill's Pub and Brewery
90 Elliot Street
Brattleboro, VT 05301
(802) 254-2553
https://www.facebook.com/McNeillsBrewery/

That was then: Ray McNeill and his wife, Holiday, celebrated their pub's tenth anniversary in 1996. It's a hands-down favorite among my Internet friends, who say visiting McNeill's is a must if you're traveling to Vermont. . . . Kerry Byrne of *Yankee Brew News* says of McNeill's: "There's only one thing wrong with this place; sooner or later, you have to leave." And *Ale Street News* columnist Peter Terhune raved about Ray McNeill's Old Ringworm Strong Ale, tasted with fellow beer judges in a blind test: "elicited raves all around . . . very warming . . . long, deep maltiness . . . it's sexy."

As a side note, Peter Terhune and I appeared together on the David Brudnoy show on WBZ radio after the first *What's Brewing* was published. What a blast to talk beer with the premier intellectual (and controversial) Brudnoy, who once a month suspended all other talk to chat about beer over the airwaves.

This is now: Their Facebook page is lit up with praise from people who still love the live music, the homey atmosphere, and, of course, the beers. Not sure who is writing their posts, but a recent one boasted their use of 6 different base malts from as many countries, 5 different yeast strains, and over 30 hop varieties. Old Ringworm is waiting for you.

Northshire Brewery
108 County Street
Bennington, VT 05201
(802) 681-0201
www.northshirebrewery.com

The Equinox Pilsner and Chocolate Stout get the most mentions on their Facebook page, and Northshire has expanded its tour hours. Rumor has it that they might be moving to Manchester, so keep up with all the changes on their social media sites. Or drop by. Earl and Chris have garnered a lot of excitement with their personable tours, sometimes off-hours.

The Norwich Inn / Jasper Murdock's Alehouse
325 Main Street
Norwich, VT 05055
(802) 649-1143
www.norwichinn.com

This was one of my favorite places when I visited for the first edition of *What's Brewing*. Owners Tim and Sally Wilson were running this elegant inn that dates back to 1797, and Tim was brewing beers like Old Slipperskin India Pale Ale, Stackpole Porter, and Elijah Burton's Mile Ale, the latter named for one of Norwich's first settlers. The food prices reflected the cost of living in reverse: $2.95 to $7.95 would get you Caesar salad, soup of the day, creamed New England oysters, Maine crab cakes, and much more.

These days the beers are being created and brewed by Jeremy Hebert, whose brewing experience extends back 20 years, including a few at the now-defunct Golden Dome Brewery in Montpelier. See Laurie Caswell Burke's February 16, 2016, article in *Edible Green Mountains* for a glimpse into the pub and a walk down memory lane with longtime loyal customers (www.ediblegreenmountains.ediblefeast.com).

The beers are sold only at the inn, but some are offered in 22-ounce bottles for taking with you. And Old Slipperskin IPA? Still being brewed, along with Oh Be Joyful and Whistling Pig, some of the very brews being offered way back in the 1990s. Norwich and this inn are truly must-do destinations—take it from one who fell in love with the place.

Otter Creek Brewing Co.
793 Exchange Street
Middlebury, VT 05753
(802) 388-0727
www.ottercreekbrewing.com

Located in historic Middlebury, this brewery is open seven days a week, with packaged beer to go and growler fills available at the visitor center. At the pub, sit and enjoy the beer with a nice selection of light fare, including starters, salads, soup and chili (both made with their beer), sandwiches, panini (yes, that's correct: *panino* is singular and *panini* is plural, no *s* necessary), and mini-quesadillas. Made in Vermont for over 20 years, Otter Creek's award-winning beer is widely available. Check their beer finder for a store near you.

Pine Street Brewery

716 Pine Street
Burlington, VT 05401
(802) 497-0054
www.zerogravitybeer.com

Talk about a problem a brewery would want to have! Demand exceeding supply. Well, barring the process of finding a new facility (or building one), getting all the licenses, and jumping through a million other hoops, it's a problem Zero Gravity (later in this chapter) had in 2012 when they hit the wall with production capability at their St. Paul Street location, the one that also houses Brewpub at Flatbread. Names change; the quality doesn't. In the new 30 bbl production and distribution facility, there is also a full canning line, a tasting room, a retail shop, and a beer garden. Here they sell six-packs of Green State Lager and Conehead and also offer several beers in 5-gallon and 15.5-gallon kegs, with party-pumps available to go with them. Brewing honors go to Paul Sayler and head of production Justin McCarthy, with help from Flatbread's Destiny Saxon.

Queen City Brewery

703B Pine Street
Burlington, VT 05401
www.queencitybrewery.com

Friends and brewers Paul Hale, Paul Held, Phil Kaszuba, and Maarten van Ryckevorsel teamed up to open Queen City Brewery, producing a variety of traditional ales and lagers, as well as several specialty beers. In 2016 they released Old Monty Barleywine, an English-style barleywine made from a double-mash of four British malts and generous additions of East Kent Goldings hops, aged in Chardonnay barrels. It's getting great reviews from visitors to their dog-friendly tasting room. A couple months later, they brought back their seasonal Maibock, a golden Munich-style lager, which they describe as having a complex malty profile.

Rock Art Brewery

632 Laporte Road (Route 100)
Morrisville, VT 05661
(802) 888-9400
www.rockartbrewery.com

Rene and Matt Nadeau have been brewing Rock Art for nearly 20 years. I caught Rene one afternoon when she managed to get someone to step in for her at the tasting room so we could talk. "We built this place after starting out in our home, and we've been here since 2011," she said. "Matt was a home brewer and wanted to make a living at it. We started at our house with a seven-barrel system and eight fermentation tanks in our basement. We carried beer out, breaking our backs. So we rented a place, then built this one."

When we spoke, Rene told me about the seasonal beer they'd just released. "We make our Mountain Holidays in Vermont every year. It's a creamy bock lager that pairs well with all the holiday foods." Both Rene and Matt work at Rock Art full-time, one of the lucky couples who brew who don't have to have a day job. "We both do this full-time. Matt takes care of the brewery, and I run the tasting room and do the books. And one of our sons helped us out last summer." Matt makes an extensive list of beers, including the 2016 release of A River Runs Gruit in 22-ounce bottles, available only at the brewery.

Stone Corral

81 Huntington Road
Richmond, VT 05477
(802) 434-5787
www.stonecorral.com

Stone Corral wasn't open long before they moved to this locale to expand brewing capacity, a testament to their good beers. They have also expanded their kitchen so they can offer more variety in the food they serve. Try anything from a soft pretzel to a kale and spinach salad or turkey *panino* (my Italian husband would be proud that they got this correct . . . it's one *panino*, two *panini*) and much more.

In 2014 Stone Corral took honors at the Great International Beer & Cider Competition: Stone Corral Black Beer won the gold medal in the Schwarzbier & Bock category, and Stone Corral Latigo, a silver medal in the Scottish Ale & English Bitter category. In May 2016 they debuted Wild Red, a slightly sour Brett beer, and a new double IPA called Stampede. My favorite beer, just for the name? Procrastinator Doppelbock. Someone up there has my number!

Switchback Brewing Company
160 Flynn Avenue
Burlington, VT 05401
(802) 651-4114
www.switchbackvt.com

Making beer that is unfiltered and naturally carbonated sets Switchback apart from many of its cohorts. On the beer menu are Switchback Ale, Dooley's Belated Porter, Roasted Red Ale, Slow Fermented Brown Ale, and Extra Pale Ale. Founded in 2002 by brewer Bill Cherry and his friend Jeff, Switchback has grown steadily. In 2012 they began bottling with state-of-the-art equipment that keeps the beer true to its kegged origins.

I was lucky to speak with Megan, who does brewery outreach, one of the most fun jobs I can think of. She caught me up on goings-on: "We're always up to something here. We were draft only for 10 years, then began bottling, and we periodically release something other than our flagship. We released a roasted red ale in 2007, a slow-fermented brown ale, and then our porter. We got hops from the UVM hop extension project, and we made an extra pale ale which came out in the summer, and Marven, our take on a traditional Oktoberfest. One really exciting thing: We expanded our tasting room into a full-blown taproom. You can try samples as well as pints, and we have a brewer who each week tries out a new brew on a pilot batch system. So people who come here will get to try something not available elsewhere." Sounds like a reason to schedule a Burlington tour.

Trapp Family Lodge Brewery
700 Trapp Hill Road
Stowe, VT 05672-5074
(802) 253-0900
www.vontrappbrewing.com

I felt honored to have an interview with Sam Von Trapp, grandson of "the Baron" and Maria Von Trapp of *Sound of Music* fame. First we chatted about his famous family; then when I finally got on task, Sam told me all about the on-site brewery. Built in 2010, after his father Johannes finally realized his dream of brewing the lagers he had tasted on his trips to Austria, the original facility quickly became too small to produce the amount of those lagers that beer drinkers were demanding. In 2015 the new, expanded brewery opened. Visitors can try the beers and have something to eat at the DeliBakery. (He was excited, too, about their cross-country ski facility, which was the first to open "in the Americas.")

The Trapp Family Lodge occupies 2,500 acres of gorgeous grounds and consists of the hotel and restaurant. But day visitors can buy the beer to goor enjoy a casual menu at the DeliBakery. Sam proudly listed the items on the menu: "We have the wurst, German/Austrian sausages, soup with lager, salads, sandwiches, pretzels, and baked goods."

Brewer J. P. Williams, formerly of Magic Hat, makes the lagers he loves. Among them: Golden Helles, Bohemian Pilsner, Vienna Lager, Dunkel Lager, and a rotating seasonal lager. Does expansion guarantee a prize? Of course not. Brewing talent does. The Bohemian Pilsner (5.4% ABV) was the 2015 silver medalist at both the Great American Beer Festival and the Great International Beer Festival.

The Vermont Pub & Brewery

144 College Street
Burlington, VT 05401
(802) 865-0500
www.vermontbrewery.com

That was then: If you're traveling to Vermont, you have to try Greg Noonan's place. He is well-respected in the industry as a brewer dedicated to making great beer. Noonan himself gave me a tour of the brewery, which is located on the floor below the restaurant and bar. He pointed out that one of his recent beers, Thetford Red, was made with Vermont-grown hops and speculated that this local farm crop—killed by Prohibition—just might make a comeback.

This is now: Greg Noonan passed away in 2009, and his death reverberated throughout the craft beer industry. He fought for new laws that would allow brewpubs in Vermont and sought financing at a time when no one knew what a brewpub was. His pub and brewery opened in 1988. He was truly a pioneer, and his 1986 book *Brewing Lager Beer* is considered one of the bibles of home brewing.

During a visit back when my youngest child, Megan, was six years old, this was the last stop on a long weekend of slogging around a wintry countryside, interviewing and touring at several Vermont beer-makers. When we walked into the pub, Meg looked around and screamed at the top of her lungs, "Not another brewpub!!!" Then she began wailing. I thought I would be awarded a "Bad Mother" prize, but the people standing around us burst out laughing. Whew! She's now 25 and has favorite craft beers of her own. And there is no arm-twisting necessary to get her to go to a brewpub.

The food is classic pub fare, including this yummy number: Burly Beef Stew, described as a "homemade savory beef stew made with Burly Irish Ale, premium Angus steak shavings, carrots, potatoes, and onions." A huge number of appetizers are available, as well as sandwiches and a good assortment of true pub dishes: Toad in the Hole, Ploughman's Lunch, Cock-a-leekie Pie, Vermont Country Meatloaf, Shepherd's Pie, and Bangers and Mash. They do some entrees, too, and the prices are more than reasonable. In fact, I couldn't quite believe my eyes when I looked at the menu.

As for the beer, Russ Fitzpatrick has been part of the team at VPB for over 15 years, and he's stepped up to keep the brews coming. I spoke with general manager and jack-of-all-trades Steve Polewacyk, who has been there from the beginning, and he wants you to know: "We have a pilot brewery within our regular brewery, and we make over 75 different styles of beer a year. We experiment and do some unique and sometimes crazy styles. We're the only ones doing an actual dessert beer, our Mint Chocolate Stout, and we offer it with our homemade desserts like Vermont cheesecake and our brownie."

Many of Greg Noonan's classic and original beers are also still on the menu. When VPB was offering Bourbon Oak-Aged Stout one May, the brewery noted that it was the 23rd beer style to hit their taps that year. Twenty-three styles in less than five months? That's how they roll. In warm weather they boast a pooch-friendly outdoor patio.

Whetstone Station Restaurant & Brewery

36 Bridge Street
Brattleboro, VT 05301
(802) 490-2354
www.whetstonestation.com

This is a fun, fun place, where you can drink a beer in two states at once! Straddle the painted USGS line on the floor, and you'll be quaffing in both Vermont and New Hampshire. So that would be one reason to visit Whetstone, but how about 60 beers available all the time in a fire-lit dining room and bar and a water view of the Connecticut River? Beers, view, fire, and food. But wait, there's more: From May through November you can drink and dine at the rooftop Biergarten overlooking the river.

Zero Gravity Craft Brewery

Brewpub at Flatbread (formerly American Flatbread)
115 St. Paul Street
Burlington, VT 05401-8411
(802) 861-2999
www.zerogravitybeer.com

Since 2004 this brewpub's staff has turned out stellar flatbreads made in their homemade wood-fired clay-dome oven with local ingredients. The beers, like Conehead IPA and Extra Stout, an Irish dry stout, are brewed right here, too, by brewers Destiny Saxon and Paul Sayler. Enjoy all the brews, with 18 taps to choose from. In January 2016 American Flatbread was named best brewpub in Vermont by RateBeer, and in May 2016 it was described in *Imbibe Magazine* as one of the best places to drink beer in the state.

Vermont Beer Bus Tour

Burlington Brew Tours
(802) 760-6091
www.burlingtonbrewtours.com

Chad Brodsky began his beer bus touring company in 2009 and it's going strong, with three basic tours and the option to have him structure a special-occasion tour for you. Each tour includes a tasting and an in-depth analysis of at least 15 different beers, lunch at one of Burlington's top eateries, and round-trip transportation from your hotel or home. See the website for details.